THE SLOW COOK

80 modern & delicious slow-cooked recipes

THE SLOW COOK

Justine Schofield

plum. Pan Macmillan Australia

CONTENTS

WELCOME

For me, cooking and comfort have always been linked. There's nothing more therapeutic than a pot of delicious food gently bubbling away on a low heat for a few hours on a wintry Sunday afternoon. I adore it so much it felt only natural that my next book would be a compilation of all my favourite slow-cooked dishes.

My last book was all about embracing mid-week cooking and showing you how to stock your fridge, freezer and pantry for super-speedy weeknight dinners. Now, I'm continuing with the convenience factor, but slowing things right down – and indulging in the joys of preparing simple, hearty, sustaining meals from around the world with a healthy dose of family favourites.

The ritual of slow cooking is at the heart of how I fell in love with food, with most of my repertoire stemming from my French roots. My mumma Françoise and my grandmother Mémé instilled in me the art of cooking home-style dishes that are steeped in tradition – and it's this culinary legacy that I'm always eager to share with you. A lot of French dishes are based on the fundamentals of slow cooking: braising, stewing, poaching and roasting. Think beef bourguignon (a red wine beef stew, see page 134), chicken slowly cooked with mushrooms and finished with cream (see page 84), or a vibrant ratatouille. Mmmm, mouth-watering ... It's no wonder I'm so passionate about this style of cooking.

Slow cooking also forms the basis for many other cultures' cuisines. In this book you'll find some of my most-loved slow-cooked dishes from Morocco to Italy, Japan across to America. These recipes, even if they're new to you, will give you the warm, fuzzy feeling of coming home.

There is much to be said about the convenience of cooking hearty, wholesome recipes like these. They may take time to cook, but that doesn't necessarily mean they are difficult or time consuming to prepare. I've designed this book so that you can control how much attention you give each recipe, by including both conventional and slow-cooker instructions. This helps make preparing meals easy, with maximum reward for minimal effort.

The true appeal of slow cooking is the one-pot concept, which means not only less washing up but also big-batch cooking and freezer-friendly meals. Most of these recipes can be easily doubled so there will always be enough for leftovers to store in airtight containers in the freezer for up to three months. You can choose to cook these recipes the conventional way – in a traditional vessel like a heavy-based casserole dish, cast-iron pot, ovenproof sauté pan or even a baking dish – or set and forget, leaving the dish to cook completely unattended in that much-loved, clever kitchen appliance, the slow cooker. The ease of switching on a slow cooker just before you leave for work in the morning is so gratifying, knowing you will come home to a beautiful meal.

Slow cooking is also extremely cost effective. The ingredients that shine most after a long and low-temperature cook are usually the least expensive secondary cuts of meat that have more fat and a good marbling of connective tissue – like neck, shanks, shoulder, chuck, brisket, cheeks and ribs. A total 'ugly duckling' transformation happens, and the tough, underrated cut turns into an irresistibly tender piece of meat. And let's not forget all our beloved vegetables and how budget-friendly they can be when slow cooked in a creative manner. I really wanted to provide you with lots of ways to transform humble vegetables into iconic dishes that we all love to eat but don't necessarily know how to prepare. I'm talking about the likes of meatless meatloaf with a smoky barbecue glaze (see page 56), fennel polpette (see page 36), eggplant and mushroom cottage pie (see page 32), vegetable massaman curry (see page 50) and the crowd-pleasing favourite vegetable lasagne (see page 58). I also encourage you to embrace and explore cooking with dried legumes and pulses like chickpeas, lentils and kidney beans. Not only are they good for you, they're economical and ideal to bulk out a dish for big-batch cooking.

THIS PAGE TOP
Vegetable lasagne, page 58

THIS PAGE RIGHT
Stuffed cabbage, page 124

OPPOSITE PAGE TOP
Chermoula fish with roasted cherry tomatoes & tahini sauce, page 70

OPPOSITE PAGE BOTTOM
Hearty chickpea & chicken soup, page 88

SLOW-COOKING FUNDAMENTALS

There are a few general fundamentals I'd like to spotlight when it comes to slow cooking.

1. To maximise flavour, sear your meat and vegetables. Most of my recipes include this step as it always gives you a superior result. I can't stress this enough.
2. Choose the right cut of meat for your dish. Leaner cuts like fillets and loin are not ideal for slow cooking as they dry out too quickly and become chewy. Using meat on the bone gives you a more succulent and flavourful result.
3. When cooking seafood, choose fish and shellfish that won't fall apart too much – oily salmon or meaty blue-eye trevalla or swordfish are good; however, the real champions when it comes to low and slow cooking are squid and octopus, which become meltingly tender. Some must-try recipes in the book are my stuffed squid (see page 72) and octopus and potato salad (see page 62).
4. And, finally, add cooking liquid. Moisture while stewing is very important to allow the gelatine in proteins to slowly melt down without drying out. This, in turn, flavours the cooking stock, juices or broth to create a sauce with lovely depth of flavour.

THIS PAGE TOP LEFT
Beef cheek chilli, page 136

THIS PAGE TOP RIGHT
Chicken & chorizo gumbo, page 86

THIS PAGE BOTTOM LEFT
Prawn & lap cheong congee, page 66

THIS PAGE BOTTOM RIGHT
Poached pear & almond cake, page 180

HELPFUL TIPS & TRICKS

When it comes to slow cooking, if there is one piece of advice I really want to give you, it's to plan ahead. Believe me, it's worth it and the benefits are two-fold. First, you get to enjoy the food with your family and friends – as opposed to being stuck in the kitchen. And second, if you cook your stews, curries and ragus a day or two ahead of time they will taste even better. They'll also be lower in fat. Cooking fattier cuts – such as pork belly, oxtail, lamb shoulder, neck or ribs – then chilling them overnight in their cooking liquid allows the fat to rise to the surface and solidify. When you want to reheat and serve, simply scrape off the fat and you're left with the most glorious (and less oily) result.

THIS PAGE TOP
Lamb shank pies, page 166

THIS PAGE MIDDLE
Potatoes boulangère, page 48

THIS PAGE BOTTOM
Teriyaki-braised chicken with pickled carrot, page 100

SLOW-COOKER TIPS

Size and shape The slow-cooker market is flooded with models, from basic to full bells and whistles. Capacity size usually ranges from four to six litres, so if buying a slow cooker for the first time, consider how many people you're catering for. For this book I tested my recipes in a 5.5 litre capacity bowl – which is a great size for a family of four – and I prefer an oval shape to round as it's much more versatile. Oval varieties more easily allow you to fit in and cook whole cuts of meat like lamb shoulder, roasts, shanks and sides of fish.

Seal off meat and vegetables When testing my recipes, I found that initially sealing off the meat and vegetables in a large pan, then tipping them into the slow cooker produced delicious depth of flavour in the finished dish; whereas cooking everything from scratch in the slow cooker sometimes produced insipid results. It's well worth investing that extra 15–20 minutes in this step, and then transferring to your slow cooker to set and forget.

Keep in mind that every slow cooker is different Slow cookers are safe, energy efficient and usually of large capacity, so bigger quantities can be made. Each one will vary in shape and capacity, so be sure to read the instructions and get to know your machine. Remember that cooking is all about experimenting and trial and error. Some recipes will need less or a little longer cooking time, depending on the model you have.

Play to the slow cooker's strength Let it do its thing for an extended period of time. I recommend not opening and closing the lid frequently as this reduces the temperature inside the slow cooker, which means you'll need to add extra cooking time so it can get back up to the desired temperature.

Reduce the sauce Because of the high moisture build-up in a slow cooker, more often than not the sauce will be watery. That's okay. In most of my recipes I'll instruct you to remove the meat and switch the slow cooker from low to high to reduce the sauce. Or, to speed up this last step, just pour the sauce into a saucepan and reduce by one-third to reach the right consistency.

Don't only stick to savoury dishes Slow cookers are known for producing excellent meaty stews, but they can be used for so much more. Their stable and even heat is perfect for sweets like crème brûlée (see page 182) and sticky date pudding (see page 188).

Use all year round Slow cookers are not only for cool-weather cooking, they are great to use in summer as they don't heat up the kitchen the way the oven and stovetop do.

CONVENTIONAL SLOW-COOKING TIPS

Heat your cooking vessel Warm the pot, then seal the meat in batches so you don't overcrowd the pot. At this initial stage you want the meat to brown and caramelise, rather than stew.

Use one pot This minimises the washing up. Also, searing your meat and vegetables in the pot you intend to use for slow cooking produces caramelised bits on the bottom that can be deglazed to deliciously flavour your stew.

Braise at a low temperature Depending on the recipe, cooking in the oven between 140°C and 160°C is optimum for a lovely even heat. Any higher and the stew will boil, rendering the meat dry and tough. This also goes for stovetop heating: start high, then turn down to low so the stew can gently simmer.

Trust your intuition Every oven and stovetop is different, so when cooking lamb shoulder, brisket, shanks or beef cheeks, check after the recommended cooking time. If the meat is not tender or easily coming away from the bone, simply cook on low heat for longer.

Slow-cooked food is utterly scrumptious, but it can sometimes look rustic, rich and uniform. I really wanted to transform my slow-cooked dishes so they're bright and texturally appealing. As you flick through these pages, you'll notice the recipes have a contemporary feel. You too can easily jazz up your finished dishes with a flutter of colour and texture from fresh herbs, chilli and nuts or by adding vibrant sides and condiments.

So, it's time to roll up those sleeves, switch on the slow cooker or fire up your oven and get cooking. Slow cooking is clever cooking ... and, as they say, good things come to those who wait.

Justine
ox

VEGGIES

MISO & MARMALADE CARROTS

Miso and marmalade: a simple combo first introduced to me by chef Matt Moran. He spreads it on salmon, which is absolutely delicious, and something I now like to tell friends and family is my own creation! This perfect pairing also works nicely with carrots. The sweet and salty glaze makes the carrots moreish and simply irresistible.

SERVES—4–6

2 tablespoons marmalade
2 tablespoons white miso paste
1 teaspoon sesame oil
2 cm piece of ginger, finely grated
6 carrots, peeled, halved and cut into chunky wedges
1 teaspoon sesame seeds, toasted

1. In a bowl, whisk together the marmalade, miso, sesame oil and ginger until a smooth paste forms.
2. Preheat the oven to 200°C.
3. Place the carrot in a roasting tin and coat with half the marmalade and miso paste. Cover with foil and roast for 40–45 minutes until the carrot is just tender.
4. Decrease the oven temperature to 160°C.
5. Remove the foil, dollop the remaining marmalade and miso paste over the carrot and toss. Roast for a further 40–45 minutes, tossing halfway through so all sides caramelise. Sprinkle with the sesame seeds and serve.

SLOW COOKER METHOD

Follow step 1.

Place the carrot in the slow cooker with half the marmalade and miso paste. Cover and cook on low for 2 hours, or until just tender.

Follow step 5.

GREEK GREEN BEAN STEW

This is a perfect example of how simple vegetables can shine when cooked low and slow. Green beans cooked in tomato and olive oil make up a humble Greek dish called fasolakia. I've added potatoes here because they cook in the same amount of time and absorb the delicious sauce nicely. This stew can be served as a main course or a side dish.

SERVES—4

3 tablespoons olive oil, plus extra to serve

1 onion, finely chopped

2 garlic cloves, chopped

salt flakes and freshly ground black pepper

3 Dutch cream or desiree potatoes (about 450 g), peeled and quartered

½ teaspoon dried dill

500 g green beans, trimmed

400 g can whole peeled tomatoes

100 g piece of feta

dill sprigs, to serve

1. Heat the olive oil in a large sauté pan over medium–high heat and add the onion, garlic and a pinch of salt. Cook, stirring occasionally, for 3–4 minutes until the onion is softened and lightly coloured.
2. Add the potato and dried dill to the pan and turn to coat in the oil. Add the green beans and canned tomatoes and break up the tomatoes with a wooden spoon. Fill the empty can with water and tip that in too. Season with salt and pepper and bring to the boil. Turn the heat down to low, cover with the lid and cook for 20 minutes. Remove the lid and cook for a further 15–20 minutes until the sauce is reduced, thick and rich and the potato and beans are completely cooked through.
3. Serve the green bean stew in a shallow bowl with the piece of feta on top and a scattering of dill sprigs. Finish with a drizzle of olive oil and a grinding of black pepper.

SLOW COOKER METHOD

Follow step 1. Meanwhile, heat the slow cooker on high.

Add the tomatoes and water filled to the top of the empty can to the sauté pan and bring to the boil. Pour the tomato mixture into the slow cooker. Add the potato, dried dill and green beans and season with salt and pepper. Cover and cook on high for 1 hour. Remove the lid and cook for a further 1 hour, or until the potato and green beans are cooked and the sauce is reduced.

Follow step 3.

BAKED PUMPKIN RISOTTO

Going against the grain of traditional risotto making, this minimal-stir, pop-in-the-oven version is fabulous. The rice remains al dente, and that desirable creamy finish is still achieved as the butter and cheese are folded in at the very end.

SERVES—4

- 1 litre chicken or vegetable stock
- 3 tablespoons olive oil
- 1 onion, finely chopped
- 1 garlic clove, finely chopped
- 330 g (1½ cups) arborio rice
- 3 tablespoons white wine (such as chardonnay or sauvignon blanc)
- salt flakes and freshly ground black pepper
- 500 g peeled butternut pumpkin, cut into 3 cm pieces
- 12 sage sprigs
- 50 g toasted skinless hazelnuts, chopped
- 40 g butter
- 40 g (heaped ⅓ cup) freshly grated parmesan
- 100 g blue cheese (such as gorgonzola), crumbled

1. Preheat the oven to 180°C.
2. Heat the stock in a saucepan or in the microwave.
3. Heat 1 tablespoon of olive oil in a flameproof casserole dish over medium heat. Add the onion and garlic and cook, stirring occasionally, for 3–4 minutes until softened and translucent. Add the rice and stir to coat in the onion mixture.
4. Pour the wine into the dish, bring to the boil and simmer for 1 minute to cook off the alcohol. Season with a pinch of salt and pepper.
5. Add 875 ml (3½ cups) of hot stock to the dish, followed by the pumpkin, then cover with the lid. Transfer to the oven and bake for 20–25 minutes until the rice is just cooked (al dente) and the pumpkin is soft.
6. While the risotto is cooking, heat the remaining oil in a small saucepan over medium–high heat. Add the sage and fry until crisp. Stir through the hazelnuts, then remove from the heat and drain on paper towel.
7. Once the risotto is cooked, add the butter and parmesan and the remaining 125 ml (½ cup) of stock and use a wooden spoon to stir through, squashing the pumpkin through the rice at the same time. Keep stirring until the risotto is glossy and creamy.
8. Scatter over the blue cheese and crispy sage and hazelnuts, and serve in shallow bowls.

SLOW COOKER METHOD

Follow steps 2, 3 and 4.

Add 875 ml (3½ cups) of stock and the pumpkin to the dish and bring to a simmer. Transfer to the slow cooker and stir to combine. Cover and cook on high for 1½ hours or on low for 3 hours, or until the rice is just cooked (al dente) and the pumpkin is soft.

Follow steps 6, 7 and 8.

BEETROOT WITH MINT & BURNT BUTTER YOGHURT

When the cooler months hit, I can't wait to start cooking with all the beautiful winter root vegetables that are at their peak, particularly beetroot. This humble vegetable, full of sweetness and earthy notes, really comes to life when cooked slowly and tossed with dried herbs, nuts and lashings of creamy tart yoghurt made even better with the addition of burnt butter. Let's not forget the stems and leaves, which are usually discarded; they fry up quite nicely and taste similar to Swiss chard or silverbeet.

SERVES—4–6

1 bunch of beetroot (about 4–5 bulbs, weighing 1.5 kg), trimmed, half the stalks and leaves reserved

2 tablespoons extra-virgin olive oil

50 g butter

½ teaspoon dried mint

juice of 1 lemon

salt flakes and freshly ground black pepper

140 g (½ cup) Greek yoghurt

½ teaspoon cumin seeds

1 garlic clove, chopped

3 tablespoons smoked almonds, chopped

1. Preheat the oven to 170°C.
2. Place the trimmed beetroot bulbs in a roasting tin. Drizzle with 1 tablespoon of olive oil and add 80 ml (⅓ cup) of water. Cover tightly with foil and roast for 1½–2 hours until the beetroot is tender when pierced with a sharp knife.
3. While the beetroot cooks, melt the butter in a small saucepan over medium heat until it becomes foamy. Continue cooking for a further 1–3 minutes until the bubbles subside, the milk solids start to turn golden brown and a wonderful nutty aroma is present. Add the dried mint, remove from the heat and allow to cool.
4. Remove the foil and let the beetroot cool. When cool enough to handle, use your hands to peel off the skins. They will slip off easily. Quarter each beetroot, add 1 tablespoon of melted mint butter, half the lemon juice and a good pinch of salt and pepper and gently toss.
5. Whisk the remaining melted mint butter into the yoghurt and incorporate until smooth and silky. Season with salt.
6. Wash the reserved beetroot stalks and leaves (they hold a lot of sandy grit, so soak and rinse thoroughly) and finely chop, keeping a few smaller leaves to serve. Add the remaining oil to a frying pan and fry the cumin seeds and garlic for 1 minute, then stir in the chopped stalks and leaves. Sauté for 6–8 minutes, tossing regularly, until softened and wilted. Season with salt and pepper and add the rest of the lemon juice.
7. Arrange the sautéed stalks and leaves on a platter and top with the beetroot. Scatter on the smoked almonds and the reserved beetroot leaves, drizzle over the burnt butter yoghurt and serve.

SLOW COOKER METHOD

Rub the oil all over the beetroot and season with salt and pepper. Wrap each beetroot bulb in baking paper, then wrap tightly in foil. Place in the slow cooker, add 125 ml (½ cup) of boiling water. Cover and cook on high for 4–5 hours or on low for 8 hours, or until the beetroot is tender when pierced with a knife.

Follow steps 3–7.

LODGE

BRAISED FENNEL WITH CORIANDER SEEDS

This is one of Mumma Françoise's specialties. She usually serves this as a side to roasted chicken or fish. Fennel is sweet and aromatic and pairs nicely with the nuttiness of coriander seeds. Whether cooking in a pan or in a slow cooker, be sure not to skip the initial sauté in butter and oil – it really makes a difference to the end result.

SERVES—4

2 large (or 4 small) fennel bulbs, woody stalks removed, fronds reserved

25 g butter

1 tablespoon olive oil

salt flakes and freshly ground black pepper

2 garlic cloves, bruised and peeled

1 teaspoon coriander seeds, crushed

juice of ½ lemon

2 flat-leaf parsley sprigs, chopped

1. Cut each fennel bulb into six wedges; if small, cut into quarters.
2. Place a large sauté pan over medium–high heat and add the butter and olive oil. Once the butter mixture is foamy, add the fennel and cook for 2 minutes on each side until lightly browned. Season with salt and pepper, add the garlic and coriander seeds and cook for a further 1 minute.
3. Add the lemon juice and 125 ml (½ cup) of water and cover with the lid. Turn the heat down to low and braise for 25–30 minutes until the fennel is just tender.
4. Serve the braised fennel with the reserved fennel fronds and the parsley scattered over the top.

SLOW COOKER METHOD

Follow steps 1 and 2, then transfer the fennel mixture to the slow cooker and add the lemon juice and water. Cover and cook on high for 2½–3 hours or on low for 6 hours, or until the fennel is tender.

Follow step 4.

BRUSSELS SPROUTS WITH CASHEW CREAM

This is such a flavourful and hearty vegetable dish that's made even better with the addition of a little cured pork. And cooking the brussels sprouts twice transforms them into irresistible little gems. I also like to make this for my vegetarian and vegan friends: simply omit the guanciale or pancetta, fry the brussels sprouts in olive oil instead of fat and serve with chopped, toasted salted cashews.

SERVES—4

155 g (1 cup) cashew nuts

1 garlic clove, bruised and peeled

250 ml (1 cup) chicken stock

1 tablespoon olive oil, plus extra to serve

750 g brussels sprouts, trimmed and halved

150 g guanciale or pancetta, finely chopped

1 teaspoon smoked paprika, plus extra to serve

zest and juice of ½ lemon

salt flakes and freshly ground black pepper

1. Place the cashews in a bowl and cover with water. Soak for 2–3 hours to soften.
2. Add the garlic, stock and olive oil to a sauté pan and bring to the boil. Add the brussels sprouts, turn the heat down to low, cover and cook for 5–6 minutes until the brussels sprouts are just tender, but still slightly firm in the centre, and have absorbed the flavour of the oil and stock. Reserve the garlic and 3 tablespoons of stock and drain the brussels sprouts.
3. Wipe the sauté pan clean, add the guanciale or pancetta, then turn the heat to medium (do not preheat the pan as you want the fat to slowly render) and cook until it starts to sizzle. Give the pan a shake and cook for a further 3–4 minutes until crispy and the fat has rendered. Use a slotted spoon to scoop out the guanciale or pancetta and place on paper towel to drain, leaving the fat in the pan.
4. Heat the fat in the pan over high heat, then add the brussels sprouts and cook for 5–10 minutes to caramelise.
5. Drain the cashews and add to a small blender along with the paprika, lemon zest and juice, the reserved garlic and stock and a pinch of salt and pepper. Blend until smooth. If it's too thick, mix in a little warm water.
6. Spread the cashew cream on a plate and top with the brussels sprouts and crispy guanciale or pancetta. Finish with a drizzle of olive oil and an extra sprinkle of paprika.

SLOW COOKER METHOD

Follow step 1.

Place the brussels sprouts in the slow cooker along with the garlic, stock, olive oil and salt and pepper. Cover and cook on high for 1–1½ hours or on low for 3 hours, or until the brussels sprouts are just tender but still slightly firm in the centre when pierced with a knife. Use a slotted spoon to remove the brussels sprouts from the slow cooker; reserve the garlic and 3 tablespoons of stock.

Follow steps 3–6.

CREAMED CORN WITH SMOKED BUTTER

The first time I had creamed corn like this was at a steak house in New York as a delicious side with meats and the rest of the trimmings. Of late I've been having this sexy side with barbecued seafood or just-grilled fish. You could transform your creamed corn into a chowder-like soup by simply upping the quantity of stock.

SERVES—4–6

2 tablespoons olive oil

1 onion, finely chopped

1 garlic clove, chopped

2 cm piece of ginger, finely grated

salt flakes and freshly ground black pepper

5 corn cobs or 700 g frozen corn kernels

500 ml (2 cups) chicken stock

80 ml (⅓ cup) thickened cream

zest and juice of 1 lime

1 small handful of freshly grated parmesan, to serve (optional)

SMOKED BUTTER

150 g unsalted butter

1 tablespoon chopped chipotle in adobo sauce (including sauce) (alternatively, use 1 teaspoon smoked paprika)

salt flakes

1. Heat the olive oil in a large sauté pan over medium heat and add the onion, garlic, ginger and a pinch of salt. Sauté for 8–10 minutes until the onion is softened with a little colour.
2. Peel the husks and silks away from the corn. Cut off the kernels, sliding the knife close to and along the corn cob.
3. Add the corn kernels to the dish and coat in the onion mixture before adding the stock. Turn the heat up and bring to the boil, then reduce the heat to low and cook, partially covered with the lid, for 35–40 minutes until most of the liquid has evaporated and the corn is tender.
4. Add the thickened cream to the pan and cook for a further 5 minutes.
5. In the meantime, to make the smoked butter, melt the butter in a small saucepan over medium heat until foamy. Continue to cook for 1–3 minutes until the bubbles subside, the milk solids start to turn golden and there is a wonderful nutty aroma. Remove from the heat and add the chipotle in adobo (or paprika) and a pinch of salt.
6. Ladle one-third of the corn mixture into a blender and blend until smooth, then pour back into the pan. Alternatively, use a hand-held blender and pulse five or six times to partially puree. Add the lime juice and a pinch of pepper and mix through.
7. Place the creamed corn in a serving bowl and pour over the smoked butter. Serve with the lime zest and parmesan (if using).

SLOW COOKER METHOD

Follow steps 1 and 2, then pour the onion mixture into the slow cooker and add the corn kernels. Coat the corn in the onion mixture and pour in the stock. Cover and cook on high for 2½–3 hours or on low for 4½–5 hours.

Add the thickened cream to the corn mixture and cook, uncovered, on high for a further 20 minutes.

Follow steps 5, 6 and 7.

EGGPLANT & MUSHROOM COTTAGE PIE

We usually associate a hearty cottage pie with a meat filling but eggplant and mushroom make a great vegetable substitute. This dish is not only loved by my vegetarian connoisseurs but by my meat-loving family and friends too.

SERVES—6

30 g dried porcini mushrooms

2 eggplants (about 800 g), peeled and cut into 3 cm cubes

salt flakes and freshly ground black pepper

125 ml (1/2 cup) olive oil

1 onion, chopped

1 carrot, grated

3 garlic cloves, chopped

1/2 teaspoon chilli flakes

1 cinnamon stick

2 rosemary sprigs, leaves picked and chopped, plus extra to serve

400 g mixed mushrooms (such as button, shiitake, oyster), roughly chopped

2 tablespoons tomato paste

250 ml (1 cup) red wine (such as shiraz or cabernet sauvignon)

400 g can whole peeled tomatoes, juices drained and tomatoes crushed

50 g walnuts, finely chopped

20 g parmesan, finely grated

MASH

6 desiree potatoes (about 1 kg), peeled and quartered

salt flakes and freshly ground black pepper

50 g butter

180 ml (3/4 cup) milk

1. Soak the porcini mushrooms in 500 ml (2 cups) of hot water for 15 minutes to rehydrate.
2. Toss the eggplant and 1 tablespoon of salt together and stand in a colander for 30 minutes to soften and drain slightly. Rinse the salt off the eggplant, then pat dry with paper towel.
3. Heat a large, heavy-based sauté pan over high heat. Add 2 tablespoons of olive oil and half the eggplant and fry for 5–6 minutes until the eggplant is golden. Set aside on a plate and repeat with more oil and the rest of the eggplant. Add the remaining oil, the onion, carrot, garlic, chilli flakes, cinnamon and chopped rosemary and cook over medium heat for 3–4 minutes to soften. Stir in the mixed mushroom and coat in the onion mixture, then cook, stirring occasionally, for 3–4 minutes to soften and get some colour on the mushroom. Add the tomato paste and cook for 2 minutes to darken slightly. Deglaze with the wine and simmer until reduced by at least one-third. Add the crushed tomatoes. Roughly chop the porcini and add along with the soaking liquid, leaving the sediment at the bottom of the bowl. Stir through.
4. Return the eggplant to the pan and add a pinch of pepper. Cover, reduce the heat to low and simmer, stirring occasionally, for 1 hour, or until the ragu is thick and rich.
5. Meanwhile, to make the mash, place the potato in a large saucepan, cover with cold water and add a good pinch of salt. Bring to the boil, then cook for 20 minutes until the potato is soft. Drain in a colander and allow the steam to dissipate. Return the potato to the pan and mash, then add the butter and mash through. Pour in the milk and whip with a wooden spoon until a smooth thick mash forms. Check the seasoning and add a pinch of pepper.
6. Preheat the oven to 200°C.
7. Pour the eggplant ragu into a 2 litre capacity casserole dish. Dollop the mash over the top. Sprinkle over the walnuts and parmesan and scatter on the extra rosemary. Place the dish on a baking tray and bake for 25–30 minutes until golden on top.

SLOW COOKER METHOD

Follow steps 1, 2 and 3.

Pour the mushroom mixture into the slow cooker along with the eggplant. Season with salt and pepper, cover and cook on high for 4 hours or on low for 7–8 hours, or until the ragu is thick and rich.

Follow steps 5, 6 and 7.

SLOW-BAKED SWEET POTATO WITH SMOKED TOFU CREAM

I used to avoid tofu whenever possible but after developing fun ways to use it with flavours like chipotle in adobo sauce and lime, I have a new-found love for it. It's a wonderful carrier of flavour and a great vegan alternative to dairy when you're still wanting that creamy effect. Pair with slow-baked whole sweet potato and it's a winner.

SERVES—4

4 small–medium sweet potatoes (each 350–400 g), washed and patted dry

2 tablespoons extra-virgin olive oil, plus extra for drizzling

salt flakes and freshly ground black pepper

80 g (1 cup) natural corn chips

lime wedges, to serve

smoked paprika, to serve

SMOKED TOFU CREAM

300 g packet silken tofu, drained

1 tablespoon chopped chipotle in adobo sauce (including sauce)

zest and juice of 1 lime

1 garlic clove, finely chopped

1 teaspoon brown sugar

1 spring onion, white part roughly chopped, green part finely chopped

salt flakes and freshly ground black pepper

1. To start on the smoked tofu cream, wrap the tofu in paper towel or a clean cloth and place on a small plate. Weigh down by placing another small plate on top, then refrigerate for at least 2 hours to drain as much liquid as possible. You can do this step the day before.
2. Preheat the oven to 150°C. Line a baking tray with foil, then baking paper. Arrange the sweet potatoes on the prepared tray, rub all over with the olive oil, then season with salt and pepper.
3. Bake the sweet potatoes for 2 hours or so, turning halfway through, until soft when the thickest part is pierced with the tip of a knife. (The cooking time will vary depending on the size of your sweet potatoes.)
4. To finish the smoked tofu cream, place the drained tofu in a small blender, add the chipotle in adobo sauce, lime zest and juice, garlic, brown sugar and spring onion white part and whiz until smooth. Season with a good pinch of salt and pepper.
5. Spread the smoked tofu cream on a platter, then cut the sweet potatoes on an angle into thick slices and arrange on top. Drizzle with the extra olive oil, scatter over the spring onion green part and serve with the corn chips, lime wedges and a sprinkle of smoked paprika.

SLOW COOKER METHOD

Follow steps 1 and 4 for the smoked tofu cream.

Rub the oil all over the sweet potatoes and season with salt and pepper. Wrap each sweet potato in baking paper, then wrap tightly in foil. Place in the slow cooker and cover with the lid. Cook on high for 4 hours or on low for 8 hours, or until the thickest part of a sweet potato is tender when pierced with a knife.

Follow step 5.

FENNEL POLPETTE

Meatless meatballs? Yes, they can be done and they work a treat! I tried these in the south of Italy a few years ago and have since recreated them at home. Initially, you'll think it's not possible for fennel to form polpette, but after blending with the breadcrumbs, parmesan and ricotta they hold their shape well. They are truly delicious and great served simply with toasted sourdough, but if you want to make this into a bigger meal, serve with pasta.

SERVES—4

1 large fennel bulb (about 500 g), cut into 6 wedges, fronds reserved

1 large onion, cut into 6 wedges

3 tablespoons olive oil

salt flakes and freshly ground black pepper

2 tablespoons pine nuts

160 g (2 cups) fresh breadcrumbs

60 g parmesan, grated, plus extra to serve

125 g (½ cup) fresh ricotta

1 egg

1 garlic clove

500 g tomato passata

4 slices of sourdough bread, toasted

1. Preheat the oven to 180°C.
2. Arrange the fennel and onion wedges on a large baking tray and drizzle over 1 tablespoon of olive oil. Season with salt and roast for 25–30 minutes until tender and slightly caramelised, turning the vegetables halfway through so they colour evenly. About 5 minutes before the end of cooking, scatter over the pine nuts to toast until golden.
3. Reserve half the roasted onion and add the remainder to a food processor along with the fennel and pine nuts. Pulse to finely chop, then add the breadcrumbs, parmesan, ricotta and egg. Season with salt and pepper and pulse again until a rough 'mince' forms and the mixture is slightly sticky.
4. Wet your hands with water (this makes rolling easier) and shape the fennel mixture into walnut-sized balls. Place the fennel polpette back on the tray and drizzle over a little more oil. Bake for 25–30 minutes until golden.
5. In the meantime, finely chop the garlic and reserved roasted onion, place in a large sauté pan over medium heat and add the remaining oil. Add the passata and 180 ml (¾ cup) of water and season to taste. Cook, stirring occasionally, for 15–20 minutes until thick and rich. Add the fennel polpette and turn to coat. Scatter over the reserved fennel fronds and a good sprinkling of extra parmesan and serve with the toasted sourdough.

SLOW COOKER METHOD

Follow steps 1–4.

Place the garlic, passata, reserved roasted onion, remaining oil and a pinch of salt and pepper in the slow cooker. Cover and cook on high for 2 hours, or until thick and rich.

Place the cooked fennel polpette in the sauce and turn to coat. Scatter over the fennel fronds and serve with the toasted sourdough, or turn the slow cooker to low and keep warm for up to 4 hours, if desired. The fennel polpette hold their shape well at a low, steady temperature.

LODGE

POT-ROASTED WHOLE CAULIFLOWER

I love cooking and serving vegetables in their entirety. The whole vegetable always looks so dramatic when it comes to the table, yet very little labour is involved in the preparation. Cauliflower cooked whole is very tasty, particularly when served with a rich tomato sauce. I was really impressed with the slow-cooker version – the texture was perfect – so if you have a slower cooker, it's a must try.

SERVES—4–6

1 large head of cauliflower, leaves trimmed

2 tablespoons olive oil

25 g butter

1 onion, sliced

1 red capsicum, sliced

1 carrot, cut into thin rounds

3 tablespoons raisins

salt flakes and freshly ground black pepper

4 garlic cloves, finely sliced

1 rosemary sprig, leaves picked and roughly chopped

1 teaspoon caraway seeds

1 teaspoon ground coriander

1 teaspoon ground cumin

1 tablespoon sherry vinegar

500 ml (2 cups) white wine (such as chardonnay or sauvignon blanc)

200 g tomato passata

finely chopped flat-leaf parsley and smoked almonds, to serve

1. Preheat the oven to 180°C.
2. Cut a cross in the base of the cauliflower (this will ensure it cooks evenly).
3. Heat the olive oil and butter in a large, flameproof casserole dish (that fits the whole cauliflower) over medium heat. Add the onion, capsicum, carrot and raisins, season with salt and pepper and sweat, stirring regularly, for 6–8 minutes until softened and lightly coloured. Add the garlic, rosemary and spices and cook for a further 1 minute. Stir in the vinegar and wine and bring to the boil, then add the tomato passata and stir.
4. Place the cauliflower, base down, in the dish and spoon over some of the liquid to moisten. Season with salt and cover with the lid. Transfer to the oven to braise, basting two or three times to ensure the cauliflower absorbs as much flavour as possible, for 1½ hours, or until tender.
5. Carefully remove the cauliflower from the dish and place on a chopping board. Pour the sauce into a shallow serving dish and rest the cauliflower on top. Scatter on the parsley and smoked almonds.

SLOW COOKER METHOD

Follow steps 2 and 3, then pour the onion mixture into the slow cooker and place the cauliflower, base down, on top. Spoon over some of the liquid to moisten. Season with salt, cover and cook on high for 3–4 hours until the cauliflower is tender.

Follow step 5.

JAPANESE EGGPLANT

This is my favourite way to cook eggplant. By cooking it twice you get that silky and soft eggplant from the first slow cook – where the eggplant is essentially steamed in the oven or the slow cooker – and then, in the second cook, it is caramelised with the sweet, sticky sauce. It may not be the traditional Japanese way of cooking this famous dish, but it is just as delicious.

SERVES—6

6 long Japanese eggplants, halved, or 2 large eggplants, each cut into 6 long wedges

125 ml (1/2 cup) grapeseed oil

salt flakes

MISO SAUCE

80 g white miso paste

2 tablespoons sake

2 tablespoons mirin

1 tablespoon soy sauce

1 tablespoon honey

1. Preheat the oven to 160°C.
2. Place the eggplant on a large baking tray in a single layer. Brush generously with the oil and season with salt.
3. Cover the tray with foil and roast the eggplant for 70–80 minutes until meltingly tender.
4. Increase the oven temperature to 220°C.
5. Meanwhile, place all the sauce ingredients in a bowl, add 2 tablespoons of water and whisk together.
6. Drizzle the sauce over the eggplant and return to the oven to roast, uncovered, for a further 20–25 minutes until the eggplant is caramelised and sticky.

SLOW COOKER METHOD

Brush the eggplant generously with the oil and season with salt. Place the eggplant in the slow cooker, ideally in a single layer, but if a few wedges overlap, that's okay. Cover and cook on low for 3–3½ hours until tender.

Follow steps 4 and 5.

Carefully transfer the eggplant to a baking tray and follow step 6.

LEGUME STEW

This is my take on a chilli con carne without the meat. And, dare I say, it tastes even better! The inclusion of mushrooms and beer makes it extra savoury and the combination of dried beans and lentils means it is both hearty and economical. I love making this big-batch recipe as it freezes and reheats really well.

Serve in shallow bowls with a dollop of yoghurt, some toasted or grilled sourdough and garnishes such as avocado, pickled onion and herbs. It's also a fantastic filling for good old tacos.

SERVES—4–6

2 tablespoons olive oil
1 onion, finely chopped
2 garlic cloves, chopped
2 cm piece of ginger, finely grated
1 red capsicum, deseeded and finely chopped
1 carrot, grated
2 field mushrooms (about 160 g), chopped
50 g chopped chipotle in adobo sauce, plus 2 teaspoons sauce
1 tablespoon ground cumin
1 tablespoon ground coriander
½ teaspoon ground cinnamon
100 g (½ cup) dried kidney or borlotti beans, soaked in water overnight, then drained and rinsed
375 ml bottle beer (any pale or dark ale)
400 g can whole peeled tomatoes, crushed
1 litre vegetable stock
130 g (⅔ cup) puy lentils, rinsed
salt flakes and freshly ground black pepper
2 teaspoons maple syrup

TO SERVE

plain yoghurt
avocado wedges
coriander leaves
toasted or grilled sourdough

1. Heat the olive oil in a large sauté pan over medium heat. Add the onion, garlic, ginger, capsicum, carrot and mushroom and cook, stirring regularly, for 10–15 minutes until the vegetables are very soft and caramelised. Add the chipotle and adobo sauce and spices and cook for a further 1 minute, or until aromatic. Add the beans and stir to coat in the vegetable mixture.
2. Turn the heat up to medium–high. Deglaze the pan with the beer and bring to the boil, then add the tomatoes and stock.
3. Turn the heat down to low, cover with the lid and simmer for 1 hour, or until the beans are soft. At this stage, the stew will look soupy; this is okay.
4. Add the lentils to the pan and cook for a further 45–60 minutes until the lentils are soft and the sauce is thick and rich.
5. Season the legume stew with salt and pepper and mix in the maple syrup. Serve with some yoghurt, avocado wedges, coriander leaves and sourdough on the side.

SLOW COOKER METHOD

Follow steps 1 and 2, then transfer the vegetable and bean mixture to the slow cooker. Cover and cook on high for 3–4 hours. Add the lentils and continue to cook on high for 2 hours until the beans and lentils are soft.

Follow step 5.

RIBOLLITA

Traditionally this soup is made with the purpose of using up whatever vegetables, stale bread and spare canned and/or dried pulses you have hanging around. In fact, ribollita in Italian means to 'reboil', which makes perfect sense as I find this tastes even better the next day.

SERVES—4

80 ml (⅓ cup) olive oil

200 g pancetta, finely chopped (omit if you'd like to keep this vegetarian)

½ teaspoon chilli flakes

1 onion, finely chopped

2 garlic cloves, finely chopped

2 carrots, finely chopped

2 celery stalks, finely chopped

1 small rosemary sprig

salt flakes and freshly ground black pepper

3 tablespoons white wine (such as chardonnay or sauvignon blanc)

400 g can whole peeled tomatoes, juices drained and tomatoes crushed

400 g can cannellini beans, drained and rinsed

65 g (½ cup) frozen baby peas

2 zucchini, diced

4 kale leaves, central stalks removed, leaves chopped

½ sourdough loaf (ideally a few days old), torn into 4 cm chunks

finely grated parmesan and extra-virgin olive oil, to serve

1. Heat 2 tablespoons of olive oil in a large, heavy-based saucepan over medium–high heat, add the pancetta, chilli flakes, onion and garlic and cook for 2–3 minutes to soften. Add the carrot, celery, rosemary and salt and pepper and cook, stirring regularly, for 5 minutes. Add the wine and reduce by one-third before adding the tomatoes, cannellini beans and peas.
2. Add 2 litres of hot water to the pan and bring to the boil. Check the seasoning, then turn the heat down to low, cover with the lid and cook for 30 minutes. Add the zucchini, kale and one-third of the bread and cook for a further 15 minutes, or until the vegetables are tender.
3. While the soup is cooking, preheat the oven to 180°C. Place the remaining bread on a baking tray, drizzle over the remaining olive oil and season with salt. Toast in the oven for 10–15 minutes until crunchy and golden.
4. When you are almost ready to serve, remove the pan from the heat and nestle the crusty bread halfway into the soup. Let the soup stand for 10 minutes, then serve with the parmesan, some more pepper and a splash of extra-virgin olive oil.

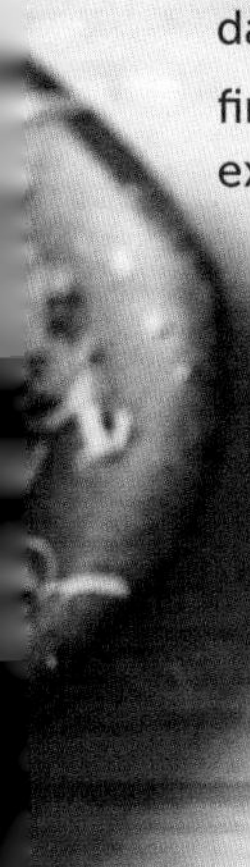

SLOW COOKER METHOD

Follow step 1, then transfer the mixture to the slow cooker. Add the zucchini, kale, 2 litres of water and one-third of the bread. Cover and cook on high for 3 hours or on low for 6 hours.

Follow steps 3 and 4.

STUFFED ONIONS

Onions are so versatile – I really wanted to highlight this hero ingredient and show that it is more than just a base to sauces and stews. Here, they are stuffed with couscous and cheese to make them into a filling meal. When you slow cook whole onions, they go from being overly pungent to sweet, soft and aromatic.

SERVES—2–4

8 red onions, unpeeled

3 tablespoons boiling water

3 tablespoons instant couscous

1 tablespoon capers, drained and finely chopped

zest of 1 lemon

3 thyme sprigs, leaves picked and finely chopped

100 g (½ cup) fresh ricotta

40 g (½ cup) grated pecorino

salt flakes and freshly ground black pepper

1 tablespoon olive oil

rocket leaves, to serve

1. Preheat the oven to 180°C. Wrap each onion, skin and all, in foil and place on a baking tray. Bake for 30–40 minutes until tender when pierced through the centre with a knife.
2. Set the onions aside until cool enough to handle, then remove them from the foil and use a sharp knife to slice the top off each one. Reserve the tops. Use your hands or a teaspoon to carefully remove the skins. Scoop out a few layers from the centre of each onion, ensuring you leave a 1.5 cm thick layer of onion around the edge. Finely chop some of the scooped-out onion to give you 3 tablespoons (save the rest to use for a soup or salad).
3. Increase the oven temperature to 200°C.
4. In a large, heatproof bowl, pour the boiling water over the couscous. Cover and set aside for 5 minutes to allow the couscous to absorb the water. Use a fork to fluff and separate the grains. Add the capers, lemon zest, thyme, ricotta, pecorino, chopped roasted onion and salt and pepper and mix well.
5. Fill the onions with the couscous mixture and place the reserved onion lids on top. Transfer the onions to a baking tray and drizzle over the olive oil. Bake for 15–20 minutes until the onions are caramelised. Serve with some rocket leaves on the side.

SLOW COOKER METHOD

Wrap each onion, skin and all, in foil and place in the slow cooker with 3 tablespoons of water. Cover and cook on high for 1½ hours, or until just tender when pierced through the centre with a knife.

Follow step 2.

Preheat the oven to 200°C.

Follow steps 4 and 5.

POTATOES BOULANGÈRE

Another version of a potato gratin, this combines potato and onion with stock, cheese and a bit of slow cooking to make the most addictive dish. The key to getting this right is to ensure the onion is well cooked before layering with the potato. Also, there's nothing worse than an undercooked potato, so, if need be, cook the potato a little longer. This is great as is with a salad or as a side with any roasted or barbecued meats or even stews.

SERVES—4

- 50 g butter, plus extra for greasing
- 1 tablespoon extra-virgin olive oil
- 3 onions, finely sliced
- salt flakes and freshly ground black pepper
- 3 garlic cloves, finely sliced
- 1 litre chicken or vegetable stock
- 6 desiree potatoes (about 1.2 kg)
- 1 small handful of thyme, leaves picked
- 2 tablespoons finely grated parmesan

1. Preheat the oven to 180°C. Grease a 2 litre baking dish with butter.
2. Heat the butter and olive oil in a sauté pan over high heat. Add the onion and a pinch of salt, cover and cook for 5 minutes. Stir through the garlic. Turn the heat down to low, cover and cook, stirring every 5 minutes, for 25 minutes. Remove the lid and cook, stirring regularly, for a further 10 minutes, or until the onion is softened. Transfer to a bowl. Add the stock to the pan, bring to the boil and cook for 8–10 minutes until reduced by one-third.
3. Meanwhile, cut the potatoes into 1 mm thick slices, or as finely as you can. Alternatively, slice on a mandoline.
4. Arrange two layers of the potato slices in the base of the prepared dish, allowing them to overlap slightly. Season with a pinch of salt and pepper. Now add half of the onion, spreading it out evenly, then scatter over half of the thyme. Repeat the process with the remaining potato, onion and thyme, ensuring the last layer is potato. Press down lightly to compress. Little by little add the hot stock so it has time to trickle into the gaps.
5. Sprinkle over the parmesan, cover the dish with foil and bake for 40 minutes. Remove the foil and bake for a further 20–30 minutes until the potato is golden brown and meltingly tender. Test this by piercing the centre of the gratin with a sharp knife. If it goes in without resistance, it's ready. Cool for at least 10 minutes before serving.

SLOW COOKER METHOD

Grease the slow cooker with butter.

Follow steps 2 and 3.

Follow step 4, layering the potato slices, onion and thyme in the prepared slow cooker. Top with the stock, then cover loosely with foil, pressing down on the potato mixture. Cover with the lid and cook on high for 3 hours, or until the potato is meltingly tender and most of the liquid has been absorbed.

Preheat the grill element in the oven. Transfer the potato to a baking dish or use the slow cooker dish. Sprinkle over the parmesan and grill for 4–5 minutes until the top is golden and bubbling. Cool for 10 minutes before serving.

VEGETABLE MASSAMAN CURRY

Massaman curry is a rich, slow-cooked Thai dish, aromatic with herbs and ground spices, coconut milk and peanuts. Traditionally made with secondary cuts of beef, like chuck or shin, it is just as delicious transformed into a hearty vegetarian delight. The vegetables used here are completely interchangeable, so add as many or as few as you like.

SERVES—4

2 tablespoons peanut oil

1 onion, finely chopped

100 g good-quality store-bought massaman curry paste

2 desiree potatoes (about 450 g), quartered

400 ml can coconut milk

400 ml can coconut cream

1 cinnamon stick

2 star anise

2 carrots, cut into 3 cm chunks

2 Japanese eggplants, cut into 3 cm rounds, or 1 small eggplant (about 400 g), cut into 3 cm chunks

2 tablespoons fish sauce

2 tablespoons caster sugar

juice of 1 lime

200 g green beans, trimmed

65 g (½ cup) frozen baby peas

50 g (⅓ cup) toasted peanuts

a few coriander sprigs

steamed rice, to serve

CRISPY SHALLOTS

4 red Asian shallots, finely sliced

2 teaspoons salt flakes

vegetable oil, for shallow-frying

1 tablespoon cornflour

1. Heat the peanut oil in a large, heavy-based saucepan over medium–low heat. Add the onion and cook for 3 minutes, or until softened. Stir in the curry paste and cook, stirring regularly, for 5–6 minutes until the paste is fragrant and splits, releasing its oils. Increase the heat to high, add the potato and toss to coat in the paste. Add the coconut milk, 300 ml of coconut cream, the cinnamon stick, star anise and 250 ml (1 cup) of water. Bring to the boil.
2. Add the carrot and eggplant to the pan, cover and cook on low for 45–60 minutes until all the vegetables are tender.
3. Meanwhile, for the crispy shallots, place the shallot and salt in a bowl and cover with water. Stand for 10 minutes to soak. Drain, then transfer to a tray lined with paper towel and pat dry. Heat 3 cm of vegetable oil in a frying pan to 180°C. (To test, place the handle of a wooden spoon in the oil; if small bubbles immediately appear around the tip, it is ready.) Toss the shallot and cornflour in a bowl, then, working in batches, add to the hot oil. Using a slotted spoon, turn the shallot in the oil until golden and crisp, about 1–2 minutes. Remove and drain on paper towel.
4. Make the curry seasoning by mixing together the fish sauce, sugar and lime juice in a bowl.
5. Mix the curry seasoning into the curry, then add the green beans and peas. Cook for a further 3–4 minutes.
6. Drizzle the remaining coconut cream over the curry and scatter on the crispy shallots, peanuts and coriander. Serve with steamed rice.

TIP—If you don't want to make the crispy shallots from scratch, store-bought crispy fried shallots are a fantastic alternative.

SLOW COOKER METHOD

Follow step 1, then pour the massaman curry gravy and potato into the slow cooker. Add the carrot and eggplant, then cover and cook on low for 4 hours.

To make the crispy shallots, follow step 3.

Follow step 4, then add the curry seasoning to the curry along with the green beans and peas. Cover and cook on high for 30 minutes.

Follow step 6.

SONYA'S POTATO GNOCCHI WITH SLOW-COOKED TOMATO SUGO

On my last trip to Italy I was lucky enough to spend some time cooking at a quaint restaurant called Canto del Maggio in the hamlet of Terranuova Bracciolini. I learned so much from the owner Simona and her chef Sonya, who, using only local ingredients, made the most exquisite dishes, including this gnocchi. I've tried to recreate it here in Australia with our potatoes and it works a treat. The trick to these cloud-like gnocchi is the addition of potato flour.

SERVES—6

1.5 kg desiree potatoes, unpeeled

salt flakes and freshly ground black pepper

2 eggs, lightly beaten

a pinch of freshly grated nutmeg

50 g parmesan, finely grated, plus extra to serve

75 g (½ cup) potato flour

150 g (1 cup) plain flour, plus extra for dusting

SLOW-COOKED TOMATO SUGO

80 ml (⅓ cup) olive oil

3 garlic cloves, sliced

2 kg very ripe tomatoes (such as roma tomatoes), quartered

salt flakes and freshly ground black pepper

1 tablespoon sugar

2 handfuls of basil leaves, plus extra to serve

TIP—The gnocchi freeze well – just par-boil them first, refresh in iced water, then freeze on a tray in a single layer. Once frozen, store in zip-lock bags for up to 3 months.

1. Place the potatoes and a good pinch of salt in a large saucepan and cover generously with cold water. Bring to the boil, then turn the heat down to low and simmer for 25–30 minutes until the potatoes are tender. Tip into a colander and set aside to drain and allow the steam to dissipate for 15 minutes.
2. Using a tea towel, hold the potatoes and peel off the skins. Then, working in batches, pass the potatoes through a ricer or mouli straight onto a clean work surface. (Alternatively, use a potato masher.) Make a mound of the potato, hollow out the centre and add the egg. Sprinkle over a generous pinch of salt, a little pepper, the nutmeg, parmesan, potato flour and 100 g (⅔ cup) of plain flour (you may need a little more or less, depending on the moisture in the potato). Lightly knead the ingredients together to form a soft, smooth dough. Be careful not to overwork it, as this creates dense gnocchi. The aim is to make them light and fluffy.
3. At this stage, I like to gently boil a small saucepan of water and test a piece of gnocchi by adding it to the simmering water and cooking it until it floats to the surface. Taste and check the seasoning and texture. If it is falling apart, don't worry, you just need to incorporate a little more flour into the dough.
4. Now it's time to roll the gnocchi. Dust the work surface with a little extra plain flour. Divide the dough into four even portions. Roll each portion into a 1 cm thick sausage shape, then cut into 1.5 cm pieces. Arrange the gnocchi in a single layer on a tray dusted with a little more flour. Cover with plastic wrap and refrigerate until ready to use.
5. To start on the slow-cooked tomato sugo, heat the olive oil in a large sauté pan over medium–high heat and add the garlic. As soon as it becomes a light golden colour (after about 1 minute), add the tomato and stir to coat in the oil. Season generously with salt and a pinch of pepper and add the sugar and basil.
6. Bring the sugo to the boil and cook until the tomato starts to break down, about 5 minutes. Turn the heat down to low, cover with the lid and cook, stirring occasionally, for 1–1¼ hours until thick and rich.
7. In batches, puree the sugo using a mouli; discard the skins. (Alternatively, force the sugo through a sieve or, if you're okay with skins, use a wooden spoon to break up the sauce well.) Return to the sauté pan.
8. Bring a large saucepan of salted water to the boil and cook the gnocchi in batches for 2–3 minutes until they rise to the surface. Remove with a slotted spoon and add to the sugo. Gently toss and serve in shallow bowls with the extra parmesan and basil leaves.

SLOW COOKER METHOD

Follow steps 1–4 to make the gnocchi.

Add the slow-cooked tomato sugo ingredients to the slow cooker, cover and cook on high for 4 hours or on low for 8 hours, or until the tomatoes have broken down and the sauce is thick and rich.

Follow steps 7 and 8.

ONION JAM & TOMATO TART

I love the way onions cooked low and slow transform into a soft, sweet, jam-like consistency. My onion jam can be made a few days in advance and, of course, it's delicious baked on buttery puff pastry with tomatoes, but it's also great served alongside cheese or added to a sandwich or burger.

SERVES—4–6

375 g butter puff pastry (see Note), thawed

2 oxheart tomatoes, sliced

200 g mixed cherry tomatoes, halved

salt flakes and freshly ground black pepper

80 g goat's cheese, crumbled

ONION JAM

2 tablespoons olive oil

20 g butter

4 onions, very finely sliced

6 lemon thyme sprigs, leaves picked

salt flakes

2 tablespoons caster sugar

2 tablespoons sherry or balsamic vinegar

1. To prepare the onion jam, place the olive oil, butter, onion, half the thyme and a pinch of salt in a heavy-based saucepan over medium heat and cook until the onion starts to sizzle, about 2–3 minutes. Add the sugar and mix through, then add the vinegar. Season with salt and turn the heat down to low. Cover with the lid and cook, stirring regularly, for 25–30 minutes until soft, jammy and golden in colour. Cool to room temperature.
2. Preheat the oven to 220°C. Line a baking tray with baking paper.
3. Lightly roll out the pastry to form a 40 cm × 20 cm rectangle. Roll onto the rolling pin and lay the pastry out on the prepared tray, then score a 2 cm border around the edge. Now prick the pastry within the border with a fork and place in the fridge to chill for 15 minutes.
4. Spread the onion jam over the pastry, keeping within the 2 cm border. Place the tomato slices and halves on the onion jam, overlapping them slightly. Season with salt and pepper and sprinkle over the remaining thyme. Bake for 35–40 minutes until the pastry is golden.
5. Allow the tart to cool for 20 minutes, then scatter over the goat's cheese and serve.

NOTE—Alternatively, use 1 sheet of supermarket puff pastry, which you don't need to roll out.

SLOW COOKER METHOD

To prepare the onion jam, place the olive oil, butter, onion, half the thyme, the sugar, vinegar and a pinch of salt in the slow cooker. Cover and cook on high for 4–5 hours or on low for 6 hours, or until soft and golden. If the onion is a little watery, remove the lid for the last hour and cook, stirring occasionally, until sticky. Cool to room temperature.

Follow steps 2–5.

LENTIL & BEAN LOAF

I love meatloaf so much I wanted to develop a vegetarian version that everyone can enjoy. And here is one that's a keeper! This meatless loaf is full of goodness with the addition of three pulses that you probably already have in your pantry. And, in keeping with the pantry theme, this smoky barbeque sauce – made with common condiments – really takes it up a notch and makes the loaf utterly delicious.

SERVES—8

1 onion, chopped

1 carrot, cut into chunks

10 cm piece of celery, chopped

2 tablespoons olive oil

150 g day-old sourdough bread, roughly torn

60 g (½ cup) walnuts

1 teaspoon dried oregano

1 teaspoon smoked paprika

400 g can chickpeas, drained, liquid reserved

400 g can kidney beans, drained and rinsed

400 g can lentils, drained and rinsed

200 g (1 cup) cooked quinoa

flat-leaf parsley sprigs, to serve

rocket leaves, to serve

SMOKY BARBECUE SAUCE

125 g (½ cup) tomato ketchup

3 tablespoons apple cider vinegar

2 tablespoons worcestershire sauce

1 teaspoon Chinese five spice

1 garlic clove, finely grated

tomato relish, to serve

1. Preheat the oven to 180°C. Grease and line a 1.5 litre capacity loaf tin with baking paper, allowing the excess paper to overhang the sides (this makes removing the loaf much easier once it is cooked).
2. Combine all the barbecue sauce ingredients in a small saucepan and bring to the boil for 1 minute. Stand until required.
3. Place the onion, carrot and celery in a food processor and whiz until finely chopped. Heat the olive oil in a large frying pan over medium–high heat, add the vegetable mixture and sauté for 5 minutes, or until softened.
4. Add the bread and walnuts to the uncleaned food processor and process until crumbs form. Add to the vegetable mixture along with the dried oregano and smoked paprika. Sauté for a further 2 minutes, or until aromatic. Remove from the heat.
5. Place the chickpeas and reserved chickpea liquid in the uncleaned food processor and process until smooth. Add to the vegetable crumb mixture. Add the kidney beans, lentils and quinoa to the food processor and pulse to roughly chop. Add to the vegetable crumb mixture along with 3 tablespoons of barbecue sauce. Stir to combine well.
6. Transfer the lentil and bean mixture to the prepared tin and press down evenly. Brush with half the remaining barbecue sauce and bake, brushing with the remaining barbecue sauce halfway through, for 1½ hours, or until a skewer inserted in the centre of the loaf comes out clean. Remove from the oven and rest for 30 minutes.
7. Thickly slice the lentil and bean loaf and serve with the parsley scattered over the top and some rocket leaves and tomato relish on the side.

SLOW COOKER METHOD

Follow steps 2–5. Grease the base of the slow cooker and evenly press the loaf mixture into the bowl. Cover and cook on low for 7 hours. Halfway through the cooking process, spread on the barbecue sauce.

Follow step 7.

VEGETABLE LASAGNE

If you're looking for a main meal that's not only vegetarian but a real crowd-pleaser, then look no further. This lasagne, laced with lots of cheesy sauce, is wonderful. Don't let your imagination stop at eggplant and zucchini as the main fillers for the sauce: sweet potato, pumpkin, cauliflower and broccoli also work really well. If using the slow cooker, I love to pop the veggie sauce on in the morning, set and forget and then all I need to do when I get home is make the cheese sauce and layer up.

SERVES—6

30 g dried porcini mushrooms
3 tablespoons olive oil
1 onion, finely chopped
1 red capsicum, deseeded and cut into 1 cm pieces
2 garlic cloves, finely chopped
2 eggplants, peeled and cut into 1 cm cubes
3 zucchini, cut into 1 cm cubes
salt flakes and freshly ground black pepper
80 ml (1/3 cup) white wine (such as chardonnay)
2 × 400 g cans whole peeled tomatoes, crushed
3 basil sprigs, leaves picked and torn
250 g dried lasagne sheets
40 g parmesan, finely grated

CHEESE SAUCE

100 g butter
100 g (2/3 cup) plain flour
1 litre milk
a good pinch of freshly grated nutmeg
salt flakes and freshly ground black pepper
100 g cheddar, finely grated
40 g parmesan, finely grated

1. Soak the porcini mushrooms in 250 ml (1 cup) of hot water for 15 minutes to rehydrate.
2. Heat the olive oil in a large sauté pan (the bigger the better as there are a lot of vegetables) over medium–high heat, add the onion, capsicum and garlic and cook for 2–3 minutes until softened. Stir in the eggplant and zucchini and season with salt and pepper. Sauté for 5–6 minutes until the vegetables start to break down a little. Add the wine and bring to the boil.
3. Squeeze the excess liquid from the porcini and reserve. Roughly chop the porcini and add to the pan along with three-quarters of their soaking liquid, leaving the sediment at the bottom of the bowl. Bring to the boil, then stir in the tomatoes, basil and a good pinch of salt and pepper.
4. Reduce the heat to low, cover with the lid and cook, stirring from time to time, for 30 minutes, or until the vegetables are softened. Remove from the heat.
5. Preheat the oven to 190°C.
6. Meanwhile, to make the cheese sauce, melt the butter in a saucepan over medium heat, add the flour and stir constantly for 1 minute with a whisk. Remove from the heat and pour in a quarter of the milk, whisking vigorously to prevent lumps. Place the pan back on the heat and whisk in the rest of the milk. Continue to whisk until the sauce comes to the boil and thickens. Season with the nutmeg, salt and pepper and remove from the heat. Stir in the cheddar followed by the parmesan until melted and smooth.
7. Evenly spread a ladleful of vegetable sauce over the base of a 3 litre baking dish. Drizzle over a few spoonfuls of cheese sauce, then add a layer of lasagne sheets, breaking them if necessary so they cover most of the sauce. Spread another few spoonfuls of vegetable sauce over the top and repeat the layers until you have four in total, finishing with the cheese sauce. Scatter over the parmesan.
8. Loosely place a piece of foil over the dish (ensuring it is not touching the cheese) and bake for 45 minutes. Remove the foil and bake for a further 20–25 minutes until a golden crust forms. Remove from the oven and rest for at least 20 minutes to ensure the lasagne sets.

SLOW COOKER METHOD

Follow steps 1 and 2, then pour the vegetable mixture into the slow cooker. Add the porcini mushrooms, three-quarters of their soaking liquid (leave the sediment at the bottom of the bowl), the tomatoes and basil. Season well, cover and cook on high for 4–5 hours or on low for 8 hours.

Continue with steps 5–8.

SEAFOOD

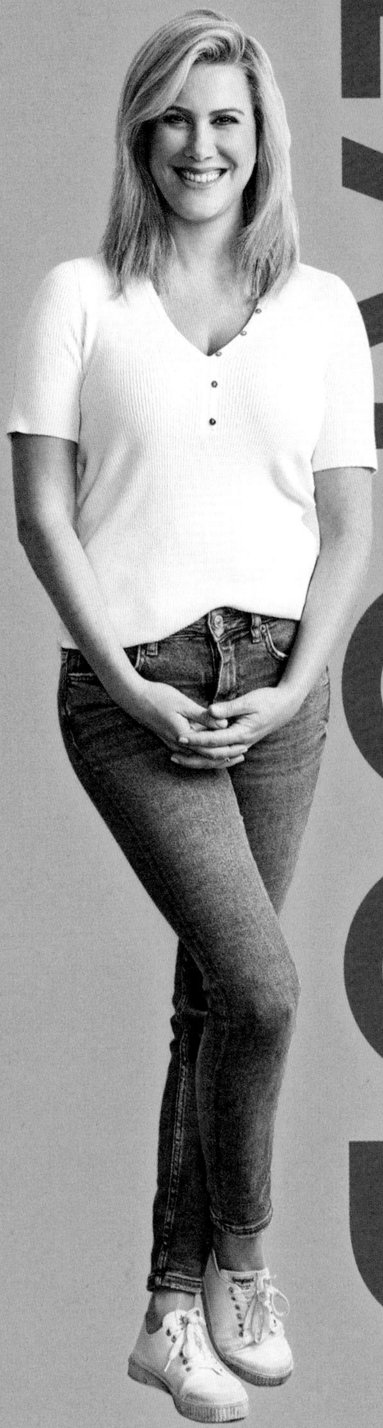

CHARRED OCTOPUS & POTATO SALAD

Octopus is now readily available at fishmongers. Next time you see it, buy it and try this recipe – it's a wonderful way to serve it. I particularly love Fremantle octopus and you can find it at good fishmongers already frozen, an added bonus as freezing fresh octopus tenderises it. Alternatively, if you have time, simply freeze your own fresh octopus.

I'm always impressed when poaching octopus in the slow cooker as the appliance maintains a steady heat, so the results are second to none. Be sure to cook the potatoes in the octopus 'stock' to allow them to take on the lovely aromatics that have developed.

SERVES—4

2 celery stalks, leaves reserved

1 onion, quartered

4 garlic cloves, bruised

1 dried bay leaf

6 black peppercorns

220 ml white wine vinegar

salt flakes and freshly ground black pepper

1 × 1.2 kg octopus, cleaned

800 g kipfler potatoes, scrubbed

2 tablespoons dijon mustard

80 ml (⅓ cup) olive oil

1 French shallot, finely sliced

1 tablespoon baby capers, drained

4 flat-leaf parsley sprigs, finely chopped

½ teaspoon coriander seeds, toasted and crushed

a pinch of smoked paprika

1. Cut one celery stalk into three pieces, then finely slice the other. Place the onion, three celery pieces, garlic, bay leaf, peppercorns, 200 ml of vinegar and 1 tablespoon of salt in a large saucepan. Half-fill the pan with water and bring to the boil.
2. Add the octopus to the pan and cover with the lid. Turn the heat down to low and poach for 45–60 minutes until the octopus is tender. To test, pierce the thickest part of a tentacle; if the knife slides in easily, the octopus is cooked.
3. Remove the octopus from the pan, place on a plate and allow to cool. Refrigerate, uncovered, for 1–2 hours to air-dry (you can do this a day ahead).
4. Add the potatoes to the poaching liquid and cook for 25 minutes, or until tender. Drain in a colander, reserving 2 tablespoons of the cooking liquid for the dressing. Set aside to steam-dry to room temperature, then cut the potatoes into even-sized pieces.
5. For the dressing, whisk together the mustard, the remaining vinegar and a pinch of salt and pepper in a large bowl, then slowly drizzle in 3 tablespoons of olive oil and the reserved potato-cooking liquid. Add the finely sliced celery, the shallot, capers and parsley. Toss the potatoes through the dressing and arrange on a platter.
6. Heat a barbecue grill plate to hot or place a chargrill pan over high heat. Rub the remaining oil over the octopus and cook for 2–3 minutes until charred all over.
7. Place the charred octopus on top of the potato salad and sprinkle on the reserved celery leaves, coriander seeds and smoked paprika.

SLOW COOKER METHOD

Follow step 1.

Heat the slow cooker on low, then pour in the poaching liquid. Add the octopus, cover and cook for 5–6 hours until tender.

Follow step 3. Add the potatoes and cook for a further 1½–2 hours until cooked through. Remove the potatoes and peel off the skins, then allow to steam-dry before cutting into even-sized pieces.

Follow steps 5, 6 and 7.

CONFIT FENNEL & SNAPPER WITH PAPPARDELLE

Slow cooking fennel in olive oil and butter really brings out its sweetness and, dotted with fish and cherry tomatoes, makes it perfect to serve as a pasta sauce. This is an elegant yet simple dish to prepare.

SERVES—2

2 tablespoons olive oil

10 g butter

1 fennel bulb (about 200 g), finely chopped, fronds reserved

2 garlic cloves, finely chopped

1 small red chilli, finely chopped

2 anchovy fillets, chopped

a small pinch of saffron threads

salt flakes and freshly ground black pepper

125 ml (½ cup) white wine (such as chardonnay)

250 g cherry tomatoes, halved

200 g snapper fillet, skin removed and pin-boned, cut into 2 cm pieces

375 g fresh or dried pappardelle

30 g slivered almonds, toasted

1. Heat the olive oil and butter in a sauté pan over medium heat and add the fennel, garlic, chilli and anchovy. Fry, stirring regularly, for 1–2 minutes until fragrant, before adding the saffron, salt and pepper and wine.
2. Bring to the boil, then cover the pan and turn the heat down to low. Cook for 20–25 minutes until the fennel is very soft and the wine has almost evaporated.
3. Turn the heat up to medium, add the tomato and cook for 2–3 minutes. Add the snapper and cook for a further 1 minute.
4. Bring a large saucepan of salted water to the boil, add the pappardelle and cook as per the packet instructions.
5. While the pappardelle is cooking, remove 3 tablespoons of starchy pasta-cooking water and add to the fennel and snapper. Bring the sauce back to a gentle boil.
6. Drain the pasta and add to the fennel and snapper. Toss well.
7. Portion the pasta into bowls, scatter over the slivered almonds and reserved fennel fronds and serve.

SLOW COOKER METHOD

Follow step 1, then transfer the fennel mixture to the slow cooker. Cover and cook on high for 1–1½ hours until the fennel is very soft and the wine has almost evaporated. Add the tomato and cook for a further 1½ hours. Add the snapper and cook for 10–15 minutes.

Follow step 4. While the pappardelle is cooking, remove 3 tablespoons of starchy pasta-cooking water and add to the slow cooker. Bring the sauce back to a gentle boil.

Follow steps 6 and 7.

PRAWN & LAP CHEONG CONGEE

On a recent trip to Macao I had congee for breakfast almost every day – I absolutely loved it. Similar to porridge but made with rice, congee is easy to prepare and endlessly adaptable. In China it's served as a breakfast staple, but I love this prawn version for a comforting lunch or dinner on a cold winter's day.

This is another slow-cooker favourite of mine, as the consistent, stable heat creates the creamiest results.

SERVES—8

- 4 cm piece of ginger, julienned
- 200 g (1 cup) long-grain rice, washed 3 times in cold water
- 2 chicken thigh fillets
- 2 litres chicken stock
- 8 lap cheong sausages (see Note), finely sliced
- 2 tablespoons soy sauce, plus extra to serve
- 1 teaspoon sesame oil, plus extra to serve
- ½ teaspoon freshly ground white pepper
- 1 tablespoon peanut oil
- 8 raw large prawns, shelled, deveined and halved horizontally
- 1 tablespoon chilli oil, to serve (optional)
- 2 spring onions, finely sliced
- crispy fried shallots, to serve

1. Place the ginger, rice, chicken, stock and three of the sliced lap cheong sausages in a large, heavy-based saucepan. Bring slowly to the boil, cover with the lid and reduce the heat to low. Gently simmer, stirring regularly, for 1¾–2 hours until the congee is the consistency of a loose porridge. Stir through the soy sauce, sesame oil and white pepper.
2. When ready to serve, heat the peanut oil in a large frying pan over high heat. Add the remaining sausage and cook for 1–2 minutes until beginning to crisp. Add the prawn meat and cook for a further 1–2 minutes until the prawns turn white.
3. Divide the congee among bowls and top with the sausage and prawn mixture. Drizzle on the extra soy sauce and sesame oil and a splash of chilli oil (if using). Scatter over the spring onion and crispy fried shallots and serve.

NOTE—Lap cheong sausages can be found at Asian grocers and in most supermarkets in the international aisle.

SLOW COOKER METHOD

Heat the slow cooker and add the ginger, rice, chicken, stock and three of the sliced lap cheong sausages. Cover and cook on high for 3 hours or on low for 6 hours. Season the congee with the soy sauce, sesame oil and white pepper.

Follow steps 2 and 3.

FISH BRAISED WITH CHICKPEAS

I love cooking with dried chickpeas – the results are far better than using the canned option – and served the way they are here, with lovely chunks of white fish, is a simple favourite of mine. I particularly love cooking chickpeas in the slow cooker as they become super creamy with steady, even cooking. Be sure not to season your chickpeas until they're cooked. If seasoned at the beginning, the outer shell will harden and they take much longer to soften.

SERVES—4

- 300 g (1½ cups) dried chickpeas (see Note)
- 80 ml (⅓ cup) extra-virgin olive oil
- 2 onions, finely chopped
- 1 fresh or dried bay leaf
- 4 garlic cloves, chopped
- 4 anchovy fillets, chopped
- 1 tomato, quartered
- 1 teaspoon dried oregano
- salt flakes and freshly ground black pepper
- juice of ½ lemon
- 600 g monkfish fillets (or other white-fleshed fish, such as pink ling, kingfish, barramundi, swordfish), skin removed and pin-boned, cut into 3 cm pieces
- 2 store-bought roasted capsicum fillets, drained and sliced
- 2 flat-leaf parsley sprigs, chopped

1. Soak the chickpeas in plenty of water overnight, then drain and rinse well.
2. Heat the olive oil in a large, heavy-based saucepan over medium heat. Add the onion and bay leaf and cook, stirring regularly, for 10–12 minutes until the onion is softened with a little colour. Add the garlic, anchovy, tomato and oregano and cook for a further 2 minutes.
3. Add the chickpeas to the pan and stir to coat in the onion mixture, then pour in enough water to submerge everything by 4 cm (about 2–3 litres but this will depend on the capacity of your pan). Bring to the boil, then turn the heat down to low, cover with the lid and cook for 1½–2 hours until the chickpeas are soft and creamy.
4. Generously season the chickpea stew with salt and a pinch of pepper. Using a potato masher, mash some of the chickpeas to thicken the sauce, then stir through the lemon juice.
5. Season the fish with salt and pepper. Turn the heat off and add the chunks of fish to the chickpea stew. Cover with the lid and allow the residual heat to poach the fish for 8–10 minutes. Top with the capsicum strips and chopped parsley and serve.

NOTE—Alternatively, use two 400 g cans of drained and rinsed chickpeas. If cooking the traditional way, cover the canned chickpeas with 2 cm of water (instead of 4 cm) and cook for 1½ hours; if using the slow cooker, cook on low for 6 hours.

SLOW COOKER METHOD

Follow steps 1 and 2, then tip the onion mixture into the slow cooker, add the chickpeas and pour in enough water to cover everything by 2–3 cm. Cover and cook on high for 4 hours or on low for 8–9 hours, or until tender.

Follow step 4, then season the fish and place on top of the chickpea stew. Cover and cook on high for 10–12 minutes or on low for 20 minutes, or until the fish is just cooked through. Serve, topped with the capsicum and parsley.

CHERMOULA FISH WITH ROASTED CHERRY TOMATOES & TAHINI SAUCE

If you think slow cookers are only for meat stews, think again. In fact, because of their consistent heat, slow cookers produce great results with the delicate nature of fish. This recipe, one of my favourites in this chapter, is a bit of a mixed bag with a North African rub for the fish and a Middle Eastern sauce, but it works nicely.

SERVES—4

1 kg cherry tomatoes

80 ml (1/3 cup) olive oil

salt flakes and freshly ground black pepper

1 teaspoon sugar

1/2 garlic bulb, cut horizontally

4 x 180 g mahi mahi fillets (or any white-fleshed fish, such as mulloway, kingfish, flathead or barramundi), skin on and pin-boned

steamed couscous, to serve

CHERMOULA

1/2 teaspoon coriander seeds, toasted

1/4 teaspoon cumin seeds, toasted

1 teaspoon sweet paprika

3 flat-leaf parsley sprigs, leaves picked, plus extra leaves to serve

3 coriander sprigs, plus extra leaves to serve

2 tablespoons extra-virgin olive oil

salt flakes and freshly ground black pepper

TAHINI SAUCE

3 tablespoons tahini

juice of 1/2 lemon

salt flakes

1. Preheat the oven to 140°C.
2. Arrange the cherry tomatoes in a large baking dish and drizzle over 3 tablespoons of olive oil, then season generously with salt, sprinkle over the sugar and nestle in the garlic. Roast, shaking the dish halfway through, for 35–40 minutes until the tomatoes are just beginning to blister and soften but are still holding their shape.
3. Remove the tomatoes from the oven and, using tongs, remove and discard the loosened skins.
4. For the chermoula, crush the toasted coriander seeds and cumin seeds using a mortar and pestle, then mix in the paprika. Squeeze the roasted garlic flesh into the mortar, add the herbs and pound until a paste forms. Add the olive oil and a pinch of salt and pepper and stir through.
5. Rub the chermoula all over the fish fillets, arrange them on top of the tomatoes, skin-side up, and roast for 15–20 minutes until the fish is just cooked.
6. While the fish is cooking, make the tahini sauce by mixing the tahini with the lemon juice, a pinch of salt and 3 tablespoons of water. The sauce should be the consistency of thickened cream. If it is too thick, just mix in another splash of water.
7. Scatter the extra coriander and parsley leaves over the fish and tomatoes and serve with the tahini sauce and steamed couscous on the side.

SLOW COOKER METHOD

Place the tomatoes in the slow cooker and drizzle over 3 tablespoons of olive oil, then season generously with salt, add the sugar and nestle in the garlic. Cover and cook on low for 3½–4 hours until the skins begin to fall off and the tomatoes soften but still hold their shape. Remove the skins with tongs.

Follow step 4. Rub the chermoula all over the fish fillets and arrange them on top of the tomatoes. Turn the slow cooker to high, cover and cook for 20–25 minutes or until the fish is just cooked.

Follow steps 6 and 7.

STUFFED SQUID

Squid braises beautifully in a sauté pan or slow cooker, which is perfect for this typically south Italian dish. After a low and slow cook, the squid become incredibly tender – and the stuffing in the squid tubes is a delicious added surprise.

SERVES—4

6 medium squid with tentacles (about 1.2 kg total), cleaned

80 ml (⅓ cup) extra-virgin olive oil, plus extra to serve

1 onion, finely chopped

1 garlic clove, chopped

3 flat-leaf parsley sprigs, stalks finely chopped, leaves roughly chopped, plus extra chopped leaves to serve

salt flakes and freshly ground black pepper

100 g fresh breadcrumbs

40 g parmesan, grated

40 g mozzarella, cut into 1.5 cm cubes

1 egg, lightly beaten

125 ml (½ cup) white wine (such as chardonnay or sauvignon blanc)

a pinch of chilli flakes

400 g tomato passata

crusty bread and lemon wedges, to serve

1. Set four squid tubes and four tentacles aside and finely chop the remaining tubes, tentacles and wings.
2. Heat 2 tablespoons of olive oil in a sauté pan, add the onion, garlic and chopped parsley stalks and fry for 2–3 minutes. Stir in the finely chopped squid and season with salt and pepper. Cook for 2–3 minutes until the squid changes colour, then pour into a bowl and cool slightly. Add the breadcrumbs, cheeses, egg and chopped parsley leaves. Mix well and check the seasoning.
3. Working with one squid tube at a time, stuff with the breadcrumb mixture, being sure not to overfill (as they may burst during cooking). Secure with toothpicks.
4. Add the remaining oil to the pan and place over medium–high heat. Add the stuffed squid tubes and tentacles and sear on all sides for 1 minute. Pour in the wine and bring to the boil.
5. Add the chilli flakes, passata and 200 ml of water to the pan and season with salt and pepper. Bring to the boil again, turn the heat down to low and cover with the lid. Cook for 50–55 minutes until the squid is tender. Remove and discard the toothpicks.
6. Transfer the squid and sauce to a serving dish, drizzle over a little extra olive oil and scatter on the extra parsley. Serve with the crusty bread and lemon wedges alongside.

SLOW COOKER METHOD

Follow steps 1–4.

Heat the slow cooker on low, add the chilli flakes and tomatoes and season with salt and pepper. Add the stuffed squid tubes, tentacles and 100 ml of water, then cover and cook for 2½–3 hours, or until the squid is tender. Remove and discard the toothpicks.

Follow step 6.

PRAWN BISQUE

My dear friend Laura Jayes, a bisque fiend, has been asking me for years to include a prawn bisque recipe in a book, so here it is! This rich shellfish soup finished with cream is the perfect dish to enjoy in the cooler months. Although it's not traditional to add pearl couscous to the classic French version, I like to include it to make it more of a substantial meal. Laura's got no excuse not to cook for me now, right?

SERVES—4

1 kg raw medium prawns
2 tablespoons olive oil, plus extra to serve
3 tablespoons pernod (or substitute with another anise liqueur, such as ouzo or sambuca)
1 onion, chopped
2 cm piece of ginger, chopped
1 carrot, chopped
1 small fennel bulb, chopped, fronds reserved
salt flakes and freshly ground black pepper
1 tablespoon tomato paste
180 ml (¾ cup) white wine (such as chardonnay)
2 tomatoes, diced
1.5 litres fish stock
3 tablespoons cream
3 tablespoons pearl couscous
juice of ½ lemon

1. Peel the prawns, discard the intestinal tract and reserve the heads and shells. Chill the prawns until required.
2. Heat half the olive oil in a large, heavy-based saucepan over medium–high heat and add the prawn shells and heads. Fry, crushing the shells with a wooden spoon, for 10–15 minutes until a deep red colour. Add the Pernod and flambé by carefully igniting with a match and then waiting for the flames to subside. Remove from the heat. Transfer to a bowl.
3. Return the pan to medium heat and add the remaining oil. Add the onion, ginger, carrot and fennel and season with salt and pepper. Cook, stirring occasionally, for 10 minutes, or until the vegetables are softened and lightly coloured. Stir in the tomato paste and cook for 2 minutes, or until darkened in colour. Pour in the wine and cook, scraping the bottom of the pan with a wooden spoon to deglaze, for 4 minutes, or until reduced by one-third. Add the tomato and fish stock, return the cooked shells and heads and bring to the boil.
4. Reduce the heat to low, cover the pan and cook for 35–40 minutes until the vegetables are soft and the soup is fragrant.
5. Transfer the soup – shells, heads and all – in batches to a blender and puree.
6. Set a fine sieve over a clean saucepan, tip in the soup and press down with the back of the wooden spoon to extract as much flavour as possible. Discard the pulp. Place the pan over medium heat, add the cream and simmer, stirring to combine, for 2–3 minutes.
7. Bring a saucepan of salted water to the boil, add the pearl couscous and cook until al dente. Drain well.
8. Add the prawn meat and cooked pearl couscous to the hot soup and cook for 1 minute. Stir through the lemon juice, check the seasoning and ladle the soup into bowls. Scatter over the reserved fennel fronds, drizzle over the extra olive oil and serve with a final grinding of pepper.

SLOW COOKER METHOD

Follow steps 1, 2 and 3.

Pour the soup into the slow cooker. Cover and cook on high for 3 hours.

Follow steps 5–8.

SLOW-COOKED HONEY-MUSTARD SALMON

Due to salmon's high oil content and delicate flesh, cooking at low temperatures ensures a succulent result every time. This is another example of how versatile a slow cooker can be. Elevating the fish from the bottom of the cooker allows it to cook evenly all over in the dry, consistent heat.

The honey–mustard combo is an added bonus, making this the perfect dish for entertaining.

SERVES—8

1 x 800 g–1 kg side of salmon, skin on and pin-boned

1 teaspoon olive oil

salt flakes

2 tablespoons dijon mustard

2 tablespoons honey

1 teaspoon gochujang (Korean chilli paste)

1 small navel orange, finely sliced

1 lemon, finely sliced

1. Take the salmon out of the fridge 30 minutes before cooking. Preheat the oven to 110°C. Line a baking tray with baking paper, brush with the olive oil and season with salt.
2. Place the salmon, skin-side down, on the prepared tray.
3. Combine the mustard, honey and gochujang in a bowl and pour over the salmon flesh, ensuring it is evenly covered. Arrange the citrus over the salmon, alternating the orange and lemon slices and allowing them to overlap a little.
4. Roast the salmon on the middle rack of the oven for 25–30 minutes until the flesh is still a deep pink and just flaking away. When small white protein bubbles appear around the side of the fish, it is cooked. (Try not to let too many protein bubbles form, as this is a key indication that the fish is overcooked.)
5. Carefully transfer the salmon and baking paper to a platter. Serve with a few salads on the side.

SLOW COOKER METHOD

An oval or square cooker is ideal for this recipe. Trim the side of salmon so it just fits into the slow cooker.

Scrunch up four large pieces of baking paper and place in the slow cooker to form a single layer. This elevates the fish and ensures it cooks evenly. (Alternatively, add some chopped onion and fennel to elevate the fish.) Line with another piece of baking paper, allowing the excess paper to go up the side of the slow cooker. Brush the paper with the oil, season with salt and place the salmon, skin-side down, in the cooker.

Follow step 3. Cover and cook on low for 1½ hours, or until the salmon is still a deep pink and the flesh is just flaking away.

Follow step 5.

FISH CURRY

I've tested this recipe on my friends and family a few times now and it always gets great reviews. Unlike other curry pastes, I've tried to keep the ingredients here to a minimum, so it's easy to put together and doesn't overpower the fish. This is everything you want in a curry – fragrant, saucy and visually beautiful with loads of turmeric and garnishes. Also, don't stop at fish; to make this into an even more impressive dish, add other seafood, like prawns, squid and scallops.

SERVES—6

- 2 curry leaf sprigs
- 1 teaspoon ground turmeric or grated fresh turmeric
- salt flakes
- 250 g (1 cup) tomato passata
- 500 ml (2 cups) fish stock or chicken stock
- 200 ml coconut milk
- zest and juice of 1 lime
- 1 tablespoon caster sugar
- 1 tablespoon fish sauce
- 1 kg swordfish or kingfish fillets (or any firm white-fleshed fish of your choice), skin removed and pin-boned, cut into 3 cm pieces
- 200 g cherry tomatoes
- 3 mint sprigs, leaves picked
- steamed rice, to serve

CURRY PASTE

- 3 tablespoons grapeseed oil or vegetable oil, plus extra if needed
- 3 coriander sprigs, roots and stalks chopped, leaves reserved to serve
- 2 cm piece of ginger, chopped
- 3 garlic cloves, bruised and peeled
- 4 spring onions, white and light green parts chopped, dark green parts julienned
- 1 lemongrass stalk, white part only, roughly chopped
- 1 long red chilli

1. To make the curry paste, pour 2 tablespoons of the oil into a blender, add the coriander roots and stalks, the ginger, garlic, chopped spring onion, lemongrass and chilli and blend until a smooth paste forms.
2. Heat the remaining oil in a large saucepan over medium heat and add the curry leaf sprigs. Fry for a few seconds (be careful as they will spit). Remove one sprig for garnish and drain on paper towel. Add the curry paste and cook, stirring regularly, for 6–8 minutes until fragrant and starting to caramelise. Add a little extra oil if the paste starts to stick. Add the turmeric and a pinch of salt and cook for 1 minute.
3. Add the passata to the pan and bring the mixture to the boil. Cook for 3–4 minutes, then add the stock and simmer for 10–15 minutes until reduced by one-third.
4. Stir the coconut milk into the curry, turn the heat down to medium–low and cook for a further 10 minutes, or until a smooth and creamy sauce forms.
5. For the spring onion curls, place the julienned spring onion in a bowl of cold water and refrigerate until ready to use. It will curl as it chills.
6. Combine the lime zest and juice, caster sugar and fish sauce in a bowl.
7. Add the fish pieces, tomatoes and lime mixture to the curry and cook for 2–3 minutes. Remove from the heat, cover and stand for 5–6 minutes until the fish is just cooked through.
8. Scatter the spring onion curls, coriander leaves and mint leaves over the fish curry and serve with a side of steamed rice.

SLOW COOKER METHOD

Heat the slow cooker on high. Follow steps 1 and 2.

Pour the curry paste into the slow cooker along with the passata and stock, cover and cook for 1½–2 hours. Add the coconut milk and cook for 30–35 minutes.

Follow steps 5 and 6. Add the fish, tomatoes and lime mixture to the slow cooker and cook for 10–15 minutes, or until the fish is just cooked.

Follow step 8.

POULTRY

BUTTER CHICKEN

Butter chicken is probably the most popular Indian takeaway, but nothing beats homemade. It's worth making the effort to grill the chicken first to get that authentic taste, and making this with thighs on the bone means you'll achieve succulent results. This is one of my favourite slow-cooker recipes as you can get all the hard work out of the way in the morning and the cooker does the rest.

SERVES—4

2 garlic cloves, finely chopped
2 tablespoons grated ginger
½ teaspoon sweet paprika
2 teaspoons ground cumin
2 teaspoons ground coriander
3 tablespoons Greek yoghurt
salt flakes
4 chicken thighs (about 1 kg), bone in, skin removed
50 g ghee, at room temperature
1 onion, finely chopped
3 cardamom pods, bruised
1 cinnamon stick
400 g tomato passata
1 teaspoon ground kashmiri chilli powder (see Note)
½ teaspoon garam masala
100 ml cream
steamed rice, mint chutney, pappadams, lime halves and mint leaves, to serve

1. Combine the garlic, 1 tablespoon of ginger, the paprika, 1 teaspoon each of cumin and coriander, the yoghurt and a pinch of salt in a bowl. Add the chicken, then cover and marinate in the fridge for 2 hours or, even better, overnight.
2. Remove the chicken from the fridge and bring to room temperature. Preheat the grill element in the oven. Line a baking tray with foil and brush with a little ghee. Arrange the chicken pieces on the prepared tray and grill for 6–8 minutes, turning halfway through to ensure the chicken is browned on both sides. The chicken will not be cooked at this stage.
3. Heat the remaining ghee in a large sauté pan over medium–high heat. Add the onion and the remaining ginger, the cardamom, cinnamon stick and a pinch of salt and cook for 3–4 minutes to soften. Now add the tomato passata, the remaining cumin and coriander, the chilli powder and garam masala and simmer for 10–15 minutes until thick and rich. Stir through 180 ml (¾ cup) of water.
4. Add the chicken to the sauce, cover with the lid and reduce the heat to low. Cook for 25–30 minutes until the chicken pulls away easily from the bone. Stir through the cream and cook for a further 5 minutes.
5. Serve the butter chicken with steamed rice, mint chutney, pappadams, lime halves and a scattering of mint leaves.

NOTE—Kashmiri chilli powder can be bought at Indian grocers, specialty spice stores or online. Alternatively, use hot paprika.

SLOW COOKER METHOD

Follow steps 1, 2 and 3, then pour the sauce into the slow cooker and add the chicken. Cover and cook on low for 8 hours, or until the chicken pulls away easily from the bone. Add the cream and cook, uncovered, on high for 20 minutes.

Follow step 5.

US

CHICKEN IN CIDER

When I want French comfort food, this is what I turn to. Slow-cooked chicken in a creamy sauce reminds me so much of my childhood. Whether you're cooking this recipe the traditional way or in your slow cooker, the results are incredible and that's thanks to cooking the chicken on the bone. If you don't want to break down a whole chicken, use a mix of drumsticks and thighs on the bone.

SERVES—4

30 g dried porcini mushrooms

1 × 1.5 kg chicken, cut into 4 pieces

salt flakes and freshly ground black pepper

1 tablespoon extra-virgin olive oil

50 g butter

8 small French shallots, peeled

1½ tablespoons brandy

200 ml dry apple cider

3 thyme sprigs

3 tablespoons thickened cream or crème fraîche

steamed waxy potatoes and steamed leafy greens, to serve

1. Preheat the oven to 160°C.
2. Place the porcini mushrooms in a bowl and cover with 125 ml (½ cup) of warm water. Steep for 10–15 minutes to soften.
3. Season the chicken with salt and pepper. Heat the olive oil and half the butter in a flameproof casserole dish over medium–high heat. Add the chicken and cook for 2 minutes on each side until golden brown, then remove from the dish. Add the remaining butter and the shallots to the dish and cook for 2–4 minutes until golden. Return the chicken and any juices that have collected on the plate to the dish and turn the heat to high.
4. Add the brandy to the dish and flambé by igniting it with a match, then wait for the flames to subside. Remove the porcini from the soaking liquid (reserve the liquid), roughly chop and add to the dish. Pour in the cider and bring to the boil.
5. Add the reserved mushroom-soaking liquid, leaving the sediment at the bottom of the bowl, and the thyme to the dish. Cover with the lid, transfer to the oven and bake for 40–45 minutes until the chicken is tender.
6. Using a slotted spoon, remove the chicken and shallots from the dish and place in a serving bowl. Discard the thyme.
7. Place the dish over medium heat, bring the juices to the boil and cook for 8–10 minutes until slightly reduced. Turn the heat to medium–low and add the cream or crème fraîche. Cook for a further 3–4 minutes to thicken. Check the seasoning.
8. Pour the sauce over the chicken and serve with steamed waxy potatoes and steamed leafy greens.

SLOW COOKER METHOD

Follow steps 2, 3 and 4, then transfer the chicken mixture to the slow cooker and add the mushroom-soaking liquid, leaving the sediment at the bottom of the bowl, and thyme. Cover and cook on high for 2–2½ hours or on low for 6 hours, or until the chicken is tender.

Follow step 6. Reduce the cooking liquid by one-third on high. Add the cream or crème fraîche and cook, uncovered, for a further 10–15 minutes. Check the seasoning.

Follow step 8.

CHICKEN & CHORIZO GUMBO

Gumbo is a Cajun one-pot specialty that I love to make as a mid-week wonder to please everyone. Traditionally, andouille sausage is used, but chorizo is more readily available and works brilliantly as a substitute. Be sure to flour your chicken first as it helps to thicken the sauce.

SERVES—4

3 tablespoons plain flour

salt flakes and freshly ground black pepper

4 chicken thighs (about 1 kg), bone in, skin removed

1 tablespoon olive oil

2 good-quality chorizo sausages (about 200 g), cut into 1 cm thick rounds

1 onion, chopped

1 red capsicum, deseeded and chopped

2 celery stalks, diced

3 garlic cloves, chopped

3 fresh bay leaves

6 spring onions, white and green parts separated, finely sliced on an angle

1 teaspoon sweet paprika, plus extra to serve

a pinch of cayenne pepper

1 teaspoon dried oregano

400 g can whole peeled tomatoes

500 ml (2 cups) chicken stock

1 corn cob, husks and silks removed, cut into 4 pieces

150 g (3/4 cup) long-grain rice, washed three times

1 tablespoon sherry vinegar

chopped flat-leaf parsley, to serve

1. Season the flour with salt and pepper. Coat the chicken in the seasoned flour and dust off the excess.
2. Heat the olive oil in a large sauté pan over medium–high heat, add the chicken and cook for 2–3 minutes on each side until golden. Remove and place on a plate.
3. Add the chorizo, onion, capsicum, celery, garlic, bay leaves and spring onion whites to the pan. Cook, stirring regularly, for about 5 minutes until the vegetables soften and begin to caramelise with the sausage. Add the spices and dried oregano and stir to coat. Pour in the tomatoes and stock (using the stock to clean out the tomato juices left in the can). Season with salt and pepper and bring to a gentle simmer.
4. Add the corn to the sauce, then return the chicken and any juices that have collected on the plate to the pan and bring to the boil. Turn the heat down to low and cover with the lid. Cook for 35–40 minutes until the chicken pulls away easily from the bone. Add the rice and stir through, then cover and cook on low for 12–15 minutes until the rice is cooked and the sauce is thick.
5. Stir the vinegar into the gumbo and season to taste. Divide among serving bowls and scatter on the spring onion greens and parsley. Serve with a sprinkle of extra paprika.

SLOW COOKER METHOD

Follow steps 1, 2 and 3.

Place the vegetable and chorizo mixture in the slow cooker and add the chicken. Cover and cook on low for 5 hours or on high for 2½ hours. Remove the lid and add the corn and rice. Stir through and cook, uncovered, on high for a further 35–40 minutes, or until the rice is cooked, the sauce has thickened and the chicken pulls away easily from the bone.

Follow step 5.

HEARTY CHICKPEA & CHICKEN SOUP

While this is fabulous cooked in a stockpot, there is something very comforting about coming home after a long day and smelling this beautiful soup gently simmering in the slow cooker. The chicken becomes incredibly tender and the chickpeas become so creamy.

SERVES—4

300 g (1½ cups) dried chickpeas (see Note)

2 tablespoons olive oil, plus extra for drizzling

1 onion, diced

2 celery stalks, diced

1 fennel bulb, chopped, fronds reserved

salt flakes and freshly ground black pepper

2 garlic cloves, chopped

2 cm piece of ginger, chopped

1 teaspoon cumin seeds

1 litre chicken stock

4 chicken drumsticks

2 large handfuls of baby spinach leaves

zest and juice of ½ lemon

80 g (⅓ cup) plain yoghurt or sour cream

3 tablespoons crispy fried shallots

chilli flakes, to serve (optional)

1. Soak the chickpeas in plenty of water overnight, then drain and rinse well.
2. Heat the olive oil in a stockpot over medium–high heat and add the onion, celery and fennel. Add a pinch of salt and pepper and cook, stirring regularly, for 4–5 minutes until softened with a little colour. Add the garlic, ginger and cumin seeds and cook for a further 2 minutes.
3. Add the chickpeas to the pot and stir well before adding the chicken stock and enough water to cover everything by 5 cm. Bring to the boil and skim off any impurities that rise to the surface. Turn the heat down to low, cover with the lid and cook for 1 hour. Add the chicken and cook for a further 1 hour, or until the chickpeas are tender and the chicken is falling off the bone.
4. Remove the chicken from the soup. Shred the meat from the bone; discard the fat and bones. Remove ½ cup of the cooked chickpeas from the soup and reserve to serve.
5. Spoon 3 ladlefuls of chickpeas and broth into a blender and blend until smooth. Alternatively, use a hand-held blender and pulse three or four times. This gives a creamy finish to the soup. If using the blender, pour the puree back into the soup. Check the seasoning; it may need a little extra salt at this stage. Return the chicken to the soup and stir through the spinach, lemon zest and juice.
6. Divide the soup among bowls and add a dollop of yoghurt or sour cream. Scatter over the crispy fried shallots and reserved chickpeas and fennel fronds. Add a drizzle of olive oil and a sprinkle of chilli flakes (if using) and serve.

NOTE—Alternatively, use two 400 g cans of drained and rinsed chickpeas. If cooking the traditional way, cover the canned chickpeas with 2 cm of water (instead of 5 cm) and cook for 1½ hours; if using the slow cooker, cook on low for 6 hours.

SLOW COOKER METHOD

Follow steps 1 and 2.

Heat the slow cooker on low. Add the onion mixture to the slow cooker along with the chickpeas, chicken, stock and enough water to reach the maximum level. Cover and cook for 12 hours, topping up with water if necessary, until the chickpeas are tender.

Follow steps 4, 5 and 6.

CONFIT OF DUCK WITH LENTILS

Duck confit, a French bistro classic, is one of the easiest dishes to prepare. You just need a little time to cure and then slowly cook (more often than not I cook this dish in my slow cooker for exceptional results). Many recipes call for a very long curing time, but I find the results too salty. My personal preference is to cure for six hours. I serve my confit of duck the traditional way with lentils and leafy greens. The best thing about confit is how the salt and fat preserve the meat for up to a month. When ready to pan-fry, simply bring the duck to room temperature and fry for crispy skin. Yum!

SERVES—4

salt flakes

2 tablespoons sugar

1 teaspoon fennel seeds

1 cinnamon stick, broken into pieces

zest of 1 orange

4 duck legs

600 g duck fat

4 fresh bay leaves

200 g (1 cup) puy or black lentils, rinsed

1 onion, halved

freshly ground black pepper

1 teaspoon dijon mustard

1 teaspoon red wine vinegar

2 tablespoons extra-virgin olive oil

2 large handfuls of watercress, thick stalks discarded

1. In a non-reactive baking dish, using your fingers, combine 150 g of salt, the sugar, fennel seeds, cinnamon stick and orange zest. Pat the duck legs dry with paper towel and rub the flavoured salt mixture into each one. Arrange the duck legs in a single layer in the dish, ensuring the salt covers the duck entirely. Cover and cure in the fridge for 6 hours.
2. Preheat the oven to 120°C.
3. Rinse the salt mixture off the duck legs and pat dry.
4. Melt the duck fat in a flameproof casserole dish over medium heat, then add the duck legs so they are completely submerged. Add two bay leaves and cover with the lid. Transfer to the oven and cook for 2½–3 hours until the meat is tender and just beginning to pull away from the bone. Cool in the duck fat to room temperature. (At this stage, the duck, submerged in the fat, can be kept in a sterilised glass container in the fridge for at least 1 month.)
5. Place the lentils in a saucepan with the remaining bay leaves and the onion and cover with 750 ml (3 cups) of water. Bring to the boil, then turn the heat down to low. Cover and simmer for 20–25 minutes until the lentils are tender. Discard the onion and bay leaves and season the lentils with salt and pepper.
6. Meanwhile, to finish the duck, heat a large, heavy-based frying pan over medium–high heat. Remove the legs from the fat, being careful not to separate the meat from the bone, and scrape off the excess fat. (Do not throw it away, it keeps well in the fridge for a few months and makes the best fried potatoes.) Fry the duck for 3–4 minutes on each side until golden and crisp. Drain on paper towel.
7. For the vinaigrette, whisk together the mustard and vinegar with a small pinch each of salt and pepper. Drizzle in the oil and whisk until smooth.
8. Serve the lentils and duck with the watercress on the side, drizzled with the vinaigrette.

SLOW COOKER METHOD

Follow steps 1 and 3.

Heat the slow cooker on high, add the duck fat and two bay leaves. When the fat has melted, add the duck legs and cover. Cook on high for 3½–4 hours or on low for 6–7 hours, or until the meat is tender and beginning to fall from the bone. Cool in the duck fat to room temperature.

Follow steps 5–8.

JAPANESE CHICKEN CURRY

Before travelling to Japan, I had no idea curry (Japanese style) was so popular. And I can see why – it's addictive! There are many different takes on the curry-flavoured stew but what they all have in common is the thick, sweet roux-based sauce that is flavoured with a small handful of spices and – that essential kitchen staple – good old curry powder.

SERVES—4–6

1 tablespoon vegetable oil

1 large onion, sliced

3 cm piece of ginger, grated

6 chicken drumsticks (about 1 kg), skin removed and knuckle cut off

50 g butter

50 g (1/3 cup) plain flour

1 tablespoon curry powder

1 tablespoon garam masala

1/4 teaspoon cayenne pepper

1 litre chicken stock

250 ml (1 cup) cloudy apple juice

1 tablespoon soy sauce

2 teaspoons apple cider vinegar

2 carrots, cut into 3 cm pieces

3 desiree potatoes, peeled and cut into 4 cm pieces

3 spring onions, cut into 4 cm pieces, plus extra spring onion green parts, julienned, to serve

pickled daikon, ginger and shallot (see Note), to serve

steamed short-grain rice, to serve

coriander sprigs, to serve

1. Heat the vegetable oil in a large sauté pan over medium–high heat. Add the onion and ginger and cook for 2–3 minutes to soften. Add the chicken and cook on all sides for 4–5 minutes until the chicken changes colour but the onion does not begin to caramelise. Transfer the chicken and onion mixture to a plate and set aside.
2. Return the pan to medium heat, add the butter and melt. Stir in the flour and cook, stirring constantly, for 3 minutes, or until caramel in colour. Whisk in the spices and cook for about 30 seconds until aromatic, then slowly whisk in the stock, apple juice, soy sauce and vinegar until smooth. Bring to the boil.
3. Reduce the heat to low, add the carrot and potato and return the chicken and onion mixture to the pan. Cover with the lid and cook for 45 minutes, or until the chicken is cooked through and tender.
4. Add the spring onion pieces to the curry and stir to combine.
5. Serve with the pickled daikon, ginger and shallot, steamed short-grain rice, coriander and julienned spring onion.

NOTE—Pickled daikon, ginger and shallot can be purchased at Japanese grocers and select Asian grocers.

SLOW COOKER METHOD

Follow step 1, then place the chicken and onion mixture in the slow cooker.

Follow step 2 and transfer the curry mixture to the slow cooker. Cover and cook on low for 2 hours, then add the carrot and potato and cook for 1 hour more.

Follow steps 4 and 5.

HAINANESE CHICKEN RICE

It was in an outdoor food court in Singapore that I first tasted this simple dish, which is essentially chicken and rice. I immediately fell in love. The chicken was so succulent, the rice so flavourful and the aromatic chilli and spring onion sauces were the perfect condiments. Don't be deterred by what seems to be a long list of ingredients; some, like light soy sauce, garlic, ginger and spring onions, are used more than once.

SERVES—4–6

1 x 1.8 kg chicken, a little of the fat trimmed, finely chopped and reserved

salt flakes

5 cm piece of ginger, sliced lengthways into 6 pieces

4 spring onions, halved

2 star anise

3 tablespoons shaoxing wine

3 tablespoons light soy sauce

sesame oil, for brushing

4 coriander sprigs

1 long cucumber, sliced on an angle

kecap manis, to serve

SPRING ONION SAUCE

3 spring onions, white and light green parts, chopped

4 cm piece of ginger, chopped

1 teaspoon light soy sauce

1 teaspoon vegetable oil

CHILLI SAUCE

2 long red chillies, deseeded and chopped

1 garlic clove, grated

1 tablespoon white vinegar

1 tablespoon caster sugar

RICE

1 tablespoon vegetable oil

2 cm piece of ginger, sliced

2 garlic cloves, bruised

400 g (2 cups) jasmine rice, washed 3 times and drained

1. Pat the chicken dry with paper towel and season with salt.
2. Place the ginger, spring onion, star anise, shaoxing wine and light soy sauce in a stockpot two-thirds filled with water and bring to the boil. Turn the heat down to low and add the chicken. Simmer for 30–35 minutes, then turn the heat off and cover with the lid. Let the chicken steep in the hot stock for 45 minutes (it will continue cooking in the residual heat).
3. While the chicken is steeping, prepare the spring onion sauce by blending all the ingredients plus 2–3 tablespoons of the chicken stock in a small blender until a salsa-like sauce forms. Taste and season with salt if required. Place in a bowl and reserve for later.
4. Combine all the chilli sauce ingredients in the same blender (no need to rinse out), add a pinch of salt and blend until smooth. Place in a bowl and reserve for later.
5. Once the chicken is cooked, remove from the stock, being careful not to tear the skin. Drain well, including the liquid in the cavity. Place on a platter and, with a pastry brush, lightly brush all over with sesame oil. Cover tightly and allow to rest for 20 minutes while you prepare the rice.
6. Using a fine sieve, strain the stock into a large saucepan and bring to the boil. Reduce by one-third.
7. To prepare the rice, place the vegetable oil and reserved chicken fat in a saucepan over medium–low heat. Once the fat has liquefied and the fatty pieces have become crisp, add the ginger and garlic and fry for 1 minute, then add the rice and stir to coat in the oil. Add 1 litre of reduced chicken stock and a pinch of salt and bring to the boil. Turn the heat to low, cover with the lid and cook for 15–20 minutes until the rice has completely absorbed the stock. Remove from the heat and let stand for 10 minutes.
8. Portion the chicken by removing the drumsticks, thighs and wings and cutting them into small pieces. Remove the breasts from the bone and slice. Arrange on a platter and scatter over the coriander.
9. Ladle the remaining reduced chicken stock into soup bowls and serve alongside the chicken, rice, chilli sauce, spring onion sauce, cucumber and kecap manis.

SLOW COOKER METHOD

Follow step 1.

Heat a large-capacity slow cooker on low. Add the chicken, ginger, spring onion, star anise, shaoxing wine, light soy sauce and enough water to just cover the chicken. Cover and cook on high for 2 hours or on low for 8 hours.

Follow steps 3–9.

PEANUT BUTTER CHICKEN

Creamy, fragrant and rich, this peanut butter chicken will be super popular with the whole family. I've tested this on my three little nieces (minus the chilli, of course, that's a work in progress) and they absolutely love it.

SERVES—4

1 tablespoon peanut oil
8 chicken thighs (about 2 kg), bone in, skin removed
1 onion, sliced
2 cm piece of ginger, grated
1 garlic clove, chopped
1 teaspoon ground turmeric
210 g (¾ cup) chunky peanut butter
2 tablespoons honey
2 tablespoons light soy sauce
500 ml (2 cups) chicken stock
salt flakes and freshly ground black pepper
250 ml (1 cup) coconut milk, plus extra to serve
1 red capsicum, deseeded and cut into 2 pieces
zest and juice of 1 lime
1 small handful of coriander leaves
1 long red chilli, sliced on an angle
50 g (⅓ cup) peanuts, toasted and chopped
1 makrut lime leaf, stalk removed, leaf finely sliced (optional)
steamed rice, to serve

1. Heat the peanut oil in a large sauté pan over medium–high heat. Add the chicken, in batches if necessary, and cook for 2 minutes on each side until golden brown. Remove from the pan and set aside. Add the onion to the pan and fry for 4–5 minutes until softened and golden, then stir in the ginger, garlic, turmeric, peanut butter, honey, light soy sauce and 3 tablespoons of stock.
2. Return the chicken to the pan and turn to coat in the onion and peanut butter mixture. Season with salt and pepper and pour in the remaining stock. Bring to the boil, then turn the heat down to low. Cover with the lid and gently simmer for 30–35 minutes until the chicken is cooked through and the sauce is thick.
3. Add the coconut milk, capsicum and lime zest and juice to the pan, stir and cook for a further 10–15 minutes.
4. Serve the peanut butter chicken with the coriander, chilli, peanuts and lime leaf (if using) scattered over the top, with steamed rice on the side.

SLOW COOKER METHOD

Follow step 1, then place the onion and peanut butter mixture and chicken in the slow cooker. Stir and pour in 375 ml (1½ cups) of stock, season with salt and pepper, cover and cook on high for 2 hours or on low for 4 hours. Add the coconut milk, capsicum and lime zest and juice, cover and cook on high for a further 15–20 minutes.

Follow step 4.

RIAD MYRA'S CHICKEN TAGINE

I was lucky enough to spend three weeks in Morocco on a food trail through some of the most magnificent cities. I'll never forget the many colourful markets (souks), little alleyways, beautiful people and the food. A particular stand-out was this very simple chicken tagine I learned to make in Fes at Riad Myra, a quaint guest house. What made it so special is the twice-cooked chicken and the use of lots of onion to create a thick, sweet sauce.

SERVES—4–6

a pinch of saffron threads

4 garlic cloves, grated

2 teaspoons ground ginger

¼ teaspoon freshly ground white pepper

salt flakes

3 tablespoons extra-virgin olive oil

1 × 1.2 kg chicken, cut into 8 pieces (or use 4 chicken drumsticks and 4 chicken thighs, bone in, skin on)

3 red onions (about 450 g), finely chopped

2 preserved lemon wedges, flesh discarded, skin finely chopped

3 coriander sprigs, plus extra to serve

3 flat-leaf parsley sprigs, plus extra to serve

100 g green sicilian olives

steamed couscous, to serve

1. Place the saffron in 375 ml (1½ cups) of hot water and steep for 5 minutes.
2. In a large bowl, combine the garlic, ground ginger, white pepper and a good pinch of salt. Mix through 1 tablespoon of olive oil to create a paste and then rub all over the chicken. Leave to marinate at room temperature while you cook the onion.
3. Heat the remaining oil in a heavy-based tagine or large sauté pan over medium heat and add the onion and a pinch of salt. Sweat, stirring regularly, for 8–10 minutes until the onion is softened and slightly caramelised.
4. Stir in the preserved lemon, then place the chicken on top in an even layer. Pour over the saffron stock to almost cover the chicken and place the herbs on top. Increase the heat to high and bring to the boil, then turn the chicken. Turn the heat down to low, cover with the lid and simmer for 40–45 minutes until the chicken is tender but not completely falling off the bone.
5. Preheat the oven grill and line a baking tray with foil. Remove the chicken from the sauce and place, skin-side up, on the prepared tray. Grill for 5–8 minutes until the skin is golden and crispy.
6. Discard the herbs and bring the sauce back to the boil. With the back of a ladle or spoon, mash the onion, then cook for a further 5–8 minutes to thicken the sauce and give extra depth of flavour. Stir through half the olives.
7. Return the chicken to the sauce and scatter over the remaining olives and the extra herbs. Serve with steamed couscous.

SLOW COOKER METHOD

Follow step 1 but using only 250 ml (1 cup) of hot water.

Follow steps 2 and 3.

Heat the slow cooker on high. Transfer the onion to the slow cooker and mix through the preserved lemon, then add the chicken and saffron stock. Turn the chicken in the mixture and place the herbs on top. Cover and cook on high for 2–3 hours until the chicken is tender but not completely falling off the bone.

Follow step 5.

Discard the herbs, mash the onion with a ladle or a spoon, then cook, uncovered, on high for 15–20 minutes until the sauce is thickened. Stir through half the olives.

Follow step 7.

TERIYAKI-BRAISED CHICKEN WITH PICKLED CARROT

Usually teriyaki sauce is used as a marinade or glaze for grilled meat or seafood. Here, I've developed a recipe where the teriyaki is used as a braising liquid – and the results are fantastic.

SERVES—4

- 3 tablespoons cornflour
- 4 chicken marylands (about 1.4 kg)
- 1 tablespoon vegetable oil
- 3 cm piece of ginger, sliced
- 3 garlic cloves, bruised and peeled
- 6 spring onions, white parts chopped into 2 cm pieces, green parts finely sliced
- 180 ml (3/4 cup) soy sauce
- 180 ml (3/4 cup) mirin
- 180 ml (3/4 cup) sake
- 2 tablespoons caster sugar
- sesame seeds, toasted, to serve
- steamed rice, to serve

PICKLED CARROT

- 2 carrots
- 1 long red chilli, finely sliced (optional)
- 125 ml (1/2 cup) white vinegar
- 110 g (1/2 cup) sugar

1. Preheat the oven to 160°C.
2. Place the cornflour in a large, shallow bowl, add the chicken and toss to coat. Shake off the excess.
3. Heat the vegetable oil in a heavy-based ovenproof sauté pan over medium–high heat. Add the chicken and cook, turning, for 6–10 minutes until all sides are golden, then remove from the pan. Add the ginger, garlic, spring onion whites, soy sauce, mirin, sake and caster sugar and bring to the boil.
4. Add 250 ml (1 cup) of water to the pan and return the chicken, skin-side up. Turn the heat down to low and cover with the lid. Cook for 1–1 1/4 hours until the chicken is cooked through and pulls away easily from the bone.
5. Meanwhile, make the pickled carrot. Using a vegetable peeler, peel the carrots into long ribbons, then cut in half. Gather into bundles and finely slice into thin strips. (Alternatively, use a julienne peeler.) Place the carrot and chilli (if using) in a heatproof bowl. Combine the vinegar, sugar and 125 ml (1/2 cup) of water in a saucepan over high heat and cook, stirring regularly, until the sugar has completely dissolved. Bring to the boil, then pour over the carrot and chilli (if using) and let the liquid cool to room temperature. (This can be done a few days in advance. Store the pickled carrot in an airtight container in the fridge.)
6. Remove the chicken from the pan and arrange on a platter. Bring the sauce to the boil and cook for 6 minutes, or until thick and glossy. Pour the sauce over the chicken and scatter on the sesame seeds and finely sliced spring onion greens.
7. Serve the teriyaki-braised chicken with the pickled carrot and steamed rice.

SLOW COOKER METHOD

Follow steps 2 and 3.

Pour the sauce into the slow cooker, then add 125 ml (½ cup) of water and the chicken. Cover and cook on low for 7 hours, or until the chicken is tender.

Follow step 5.

Remove the chicken from the slow cooker and arrange on a platter. Turn the slow cooker to high and reduce the sauce, uncovered, for 25 minutes, or until slightly thickened and glossy. Alternatively, transfer the sauce to a saucepan and reduce over high heat for 6 minutes, or until thick and glossy. Pour over the chicken and scatter on the sesame seeds and finely sliced spring onion greens.

Follow step 7.

ONE-POT CHICKEN & EGGPLANT PARMIGIANA

This is my slow-cooked take on the pub favourite, chicken parmigiana. I love this because it's a one-pot wonder with lots of different layers of flavour. Not only is there chicken stuffing, but there's tomato sauce laced with silky eggplant and let's not forget, the piece de resistance, gooey mozzarella. A true crowd-pleaser.

SERVES—4

- 4 chicken breast fillets
- salt flakes and freshly ground black pepper
- 3 tablespoons extra-virgin olive oil
- 1 onion, diced
- 2 garlic cloves, chopped
- 3 basil sprigs, leaves picked
- 1 large eggplant (about 375 g), peeled and cut into 2 cm pieces
- 1 tablespoon red wine vinegar
- 1 teaspoon caster sugar
- 3 tablespoons golden raisins, finely chopped
- 400 g can whole peeled tomatoes, crushed
- 2 × 125 g mozzarella balls, torn

STUFFING

- 50 g day-old sourdough bread (about 1 slice), crust removed, torn
- 2 tablespoons pine nuts, toasted
- 3 tablespoons fresh ricotta
- 1 egg yolk
- 1 tablespoon grated pecorino or parmesan, plus extra to serve
- salt flakes and freshly ground black pepper

1. To make the stuffing, place the sourdough and pine nuts in a small food processor and process until finely chopped. Add the ricotta, egg yolk, pecorino or parmesan and a pinch each of salt and pepper and pulse a few more times to combine. Transfer to a small bowl.
2. Working with one chicken breast at a time, place between two pieces of baking paper and gently pound to even out and thin a little. Be careful not to over-flatten. With a sharp knife, make a small incision in one side of the chicken breast to form a pocket. Use a dessertspoon to fill the pocket with one-quarter of the stuffing mixture. Press the seam closed and secure with a few toothpicks. Repeat with the remaining chicken and stuffing.
3. Season the chicken with salt and pepper and heat 1 tablespoon of olive oil in a sauté pan over medium–high heat. Add the chicken and seal for 1–2 minutes on each side, then remove from the pan.
4. Reduce the heat to medium, add the remaining oil and the onion, garlic and the leaves of two basil stalks and cook for 4 minutes to soften. Add the eggplant and a pinch of salt and pepper and stir to coat in the onion mixture. Cook for 6–8 minutes to lightly colour, then add the vinegar, caster sugar, raisins and tomatoes. Rinse out the tomato juices left in the can with 125 ml (½ cup) of water and stir through.
5. Nestle the chicken in the eggplant stew and cover with the lid. Turn the heat down to low and slowly cook for 30–35 minutes until the chicken is tender and the eggplant is very soft.
6. Remove the toothpicks from the chicken and place some mozzarella on and around each breast. Cover the pan and continue to cook for 5 minutes, or until the cheese has melted. Alternatively, preheat the oven grill, transfer the pan to the oven and grill for 5 minutes, or until the mozzarella is bubbling and golden.
7. Serve with an extra sprinkling of pecorino or parmesan and the remaining basil leaves scattered over the top.

SLOW COOKER METHOD

Follow steps 1–4.

Heat the slow cooker. Transfer the eggplant stew to the slow cooker along with the stuffed chicken breasts. Cover and cook on high for 1¾ hours or on low for 5 hours, or until the chicken is very tender and the eggplant is very soft.

Place the mozzarella on and around each chicken breast. Cover and continue to cook for 10–15 minutes until the mozzarella has melted. Alternatively, preheat the oven grill to high, transfer the sauce and chicken to a shallow baking dish and grill for 5 minutes, or until the mozzarella is bubbling and golden.

Follow step 7.

PORK

HAMMY RED LENTIL SOUP

This hearty, inexpensive soup – full of wonderful smokiness from the ham hock and creaminess from the red lentils – is one of those dishes I love to make in my slow cooker. There's no need to pre-fry anything, just throw all the ingredients in the slow cooker in the morning and when you get home, a true one-pot delight is ready for you to devour.

SERVES—4–6

1 smoked ham hock (about 1 kg)

4 whole cloves

1 Polish-style smoked sausage (optional)

375 g (1½ cups) split red lentils, rinsed

1 large onion, quartered

3 garlic cloves, bruised

2 carrots, quartered

2 celery stalks, halved

1 small handful of thyme sprigs, leaves picked

4 flat-leaf parsley sprigs, leaves picked, stalks chopped

salt flakes and freshly ground black pepper

extra-virgin olive oil, for drizzling

1. Stud the ham hock with the cloves and place in a stockpot, along with the sausage (if using), lentils, onion, garlic, carrot, celery, thyme and chopped parsley stalks. Pour over 1.5 litres of hot water or enough to completely cover the ham hock and vegetables. Bring to the boil and skim off any impurities that rise to the surface. Turn the heat down to low, cover with the lid and cook for 1 hour. Check the soup and add a little more water if it is looking too thick. Cover again and cook for a further 1 hour, or until the meat falls easily away from the bone.
2. Using a slotted spoon, carefully remove the ham hock and sausage (if using) from the pot and set aside until cool enough to handle. Remove and discard the skin and cloves from the ham, then shred the meat off the bone. Slice the sausage into rounds.
3. Meanwhile, use a hand-held blender to blend the soup until smooth.
4. Return the ham and sausage to the soup, reserving a little to serve, if desired. Check the seasoning and season with salt and pepper if required – it may be salty enough from the ham hock.
5. Divide the soup among bowls and top with a small handful of reserved ham and sausage, if desired. Serve with a scattering of parsley leaves, a drizzle of olive oil and extra pepper.

SLOW COOKER METHOD

Heat the slow cooker on high.

Stud the ham hock with the cloves and place in the slow cooker, along with the sausage (if using), lentils, onion, garlic, carrot, celery, thyme and chopped parsley stalks. Cover with 1.5 litres of hot water or enough to completely cover the ham hock and vegetables. Cook on high for 4 hours or on low for 6–7 hours, or until the meat falls easily away from the bone.

Follow steps 2–5.

PORK & PINEAPPLE TACOS

The mind-blowing flavours of sweet, spicy and tangy – from the pineapple, chipotle in adobo sauce and lime – pair beautifully here with slow-cooked pork. Delicious on its own over rice, this tasty combination really shines when served Mexican style with tortillas, sour cream and a refreshing coriander and jalapeño chilli salsa.

SERVES—4–6

1 kg piece of pork scotch fillet or boned and rolled pork shoulder, skin removed

1 small pineapple (about 1 kg), peeled

1 tablespoon olive oil

salt flakes and freshly ground black pepper

1 handful of coriander, roots finely chopped, leaves and stalks roughly chopped, plus extra leaves to serve

1 tablespoon coriander seeds, toasted and crushed

3 garlic cloves, chopped

2 tablespoons chopped chipotle in adobo sauce (including sauce)

2 tablespoons chopped jalapeño chilli in brine, plus 1 tablespoon brine

zest and juice of 1 lime

2 teaspoons sugar

12 small wheat or corn tortillas

sour cream, to serve

lime wedges, to serve

1. Remove the pork from the fridge 45 minutes before cooking.
2. Juice half the pineapple and measure out 250 ml (1 cup). If you don't have a juicer, puree the pineapple in a blender and strain through a fine sieve. Alternatively, substitute with bottled pineapple juice. Cut the remaining half into four long wedges.
3. Preheat the oven to 160°C. Heat the olive oil in a large, flameproof casserole dish over medium–high heat. Season the pork with salt and pepper and sear on all sides for 4–5 minutes until caramelised.
4. Remove the pork from the dish and add the finely chopped coriander root, coriander seeds, garlic, chipotle in adobo sauce, pineapple juice and 250 ml (1 cup) of water. Stir and return the pork to the dish, cover with the lid and transfer to the oven. Roast, turning and basting the pork with the juices halfway through, for 1½–2 hours until tender. Place the pork on a chopping board and cover with foil.
5. Meanwhile, place the roughly chopped coriander leaves and stalks, the jalapeño chilli and brine, lime zest and juice, sugar and a pinch of salt in a small bowl and stir to combine. Cover and chill in the fridge until required.
6. Preheat the oven grill. Line a baking tray with foil.
7. Brush the pineapple wedges with a little of the cooking juices in the dish and place on the prepared tray. Grill for 6–8 minutes, turning halfway through to ensure both sides are caramelised. This can also be done on the barbecue for a smokier flavour.
8. Pour the cooking juices in the dish into a saucepan, place over high heat and cook for 6–8 minutes until reduced to a thick, glossy glaze.
9. Warm the tortillas as per the packet instructions.
10. Pull the pork apart with two forks. Add to the glaze and stir to coat. Transfer to a serving dish and place the pineapple wedges alongside. Serve in the middle of the table with the warmed tortillas, jalapeño chilli salsa, sour cream, lime wedges and extra coriander leaves.

SLOW COOKER METHOD

Follow steps 1 and 2 and heat the slow cooker on high.

Add the finely chopped coriander root, coriander seeds, garlic, chipotle in adobo sauce, pineapple juice and 125 ml (½ cup) of water to the slow cooker and stir. Season the pork, place on top and turn to coat in the sauce. Cover and cook on high for 4–5 hours or on low for 6–8 hours, or until tender, ideally turning the pork halfway through but it's not essential.

Follow step 5.

Remove the pork from the slow cooker, place on a chopping board and cover with foil.

Follow steps 6–10.

BALINESE PORK

If you've been to Bali, you've probably tried their most famous dish, *babi guling* – roasted whole suckling pig rubbed with aromatic spices. Here, I've adapted the recipe by roasting rolled pork belly. The results are fantastic, as the crackling is perfect and the slow-cooked pork, spiced heavily with turmeric and galangal, is succulent. If you're making the slow-cooker version and you have time, air-dry your slow-cooked pork belly overnight in the fridge too: the drier the skin the crispier the crackling will be.

SERVES—6

1 x 1.5 kg boneless pork belly, skin scored, dried uncovered in the fridge overnight

2 lemongrass stalks, white part only, finely chopped

2 x 3 cm pieces of galangal or ginger, chopped

4 garlic cloves, chopped

2 makrut lime leaves, stalks removed, leaves finely chopped

salt flakes

1 teaspoon ground turmeric

1 teaspoon coriander seeds, toasted and crushed

2 long red chillies, deseeded

2 tablespoons peanut oil or melted coconut oil, plus extra for brushing

4 long green chillies, deseeded

2 spring onions, white parts chopped, green parts sliced on an angle

2 tablespoons fish sauce

2 tablespoons palm sugar

juice of 1 lime

lime cheeks, to serve

steamed rice, to serve

1. Remove the pork from the fridge 1 hour before cooking. Preheat the oven to 220°C.
2. Use a mortar and pestle to pound the lemongrass, galangal or ginger, garlic and lime leaves with a good pinch of salt until a fine paste forms. Alternatively, place in a blender and blend to a fine paste. Transfer 2 tablespoons to a bowl and reserve for the sambal base. Now add the turmeric, coriander seeds, red chilli and 1 tablespoon of oil and pound or blend again.
3. Place the pork, skin-side down, on a bench and spread the spice paste all over the meat, avoiding the skin as much as possible. Tightly roll up the pork, skin-side out, and tie firmly at 2 cm intervals with kitchen string.
4. Brush the skin with a little extra oil, then season generously with salt.
5. Place the pork in a large roasting tin (preferably with a wire rack in it to elevate the meat) and roast for 40–50 minutes until the skin is blistered and crisp all over. Keep a close eye on the pork and turn it every 10 minutes so it gets an even colour.
6. Pour 125 ml (½ cup) of water around the pork into the tin, reduce the oven temperature to 160°C and continue to roast the pork for 45–60 minutes until cooked through.
7. Meanwhile, return the reserved sambal base mixture to the mortar or blender and add the green chilli, spring onion whites, fish sauce, palm sugar, lime juice and the remaining oil. Pound or pulse to form a rough sauce. Chill until required.
8. Remove the pork from the oven and rest for 20–30 minutes. Remove the string, then slice into 1 cm thick pieces.
9. Serve the pork with the sauce, lime cheeks and steamed rice, with spring onion greens scattered over the top.

SLOW COOKER METHOD

Follow steps 1, 2 and 3.

Place the pork in the slow cooker, add 250 ml (1 cup) of water, cover and cook on low for 8 hours. Remove the pork from the slow cooker and air-dry on a tray for 1 hour (or, even better, uncovered in the fridge).

Preheat the oven to 220°C. Follow steps 4 and 5, then steps 7, 8 and 9.

PORK CACCIATORE

In the spirit of a traditional cacciatore (an Italian hunter-style stew), tomatoes, white wine and olives are included here, but instead of chicken I use pork. Be sure to use a fattier cut like forequarter chops so the pork stays nice and juicy; spare ribs are a great alternative, or even try diced pork scotch fillet.

SERVES—4

4 pork forequarter chops (about 1 kg) or spare ribs

salt flakes and freshly ground black pepper

1 tablespoon olive oil

1 large onion, finely sliced

2 garlic cloves, finely sliced

2 sage sprigs, leaves picked, plus extra crispy sage leaves to serve (optional; see page 22)

250 ml (1 cup) white wine (such as chardonnay)

400 g can whole peeled tomatoes

80 g kalamata olives, pitted

5 cm piece of lemon zest

crusty bread, steamed or baked rice, pappardelle or mashed potato, to serve

1. Season the pork with salt and pepper.
2. Heat the olive oil in a large sauté pan over medium–high heat. Add the pork and cook for 1–2 minutes on each side until golden brown, then remove from the pan. Add the onion, garlic and sage and sauté for 2–3 minutes to soften and colour. Deglaze with the wine, scraping the bottom of the pan to detach and mix through the caramelised bits.
3. Add the canned tomatoes and crush with a wooden spoon. Three-quarter fill the empty can with water and tip that into the sauce, along with the olives and lemon zest. Nestle the pork in the sauce and cover with the lid. Turn the heat down to low and cook for 45–50 minutes until the pork is tender.
4. Top the pork cacciatore with crispy sage leaves, if desired, and serve with crusty bread, steamed or baked rice, pappardelle or mashed potato.

SLOW COOKER METHOD

Heat the slow cooker on high, then follow steps 1 and 2.

Pour the onion mixture into the slow cooker and add the tomatoes, breaking them up with a wooden spoon. Add the olives and lemon zest. Nestle in the pork, cover and cook on high for 2½–3 hours or on low for 6 hours, or until tender.

Follow step 4.

PORK RILLETTES

Rillettes, a true French delicacy, is a way of very slowly cooking pork (or duck or rabbit) in fat, then shredding and binding it with, dare I say, more fat to form a coarse, pâté-like spread. It's probably one of my all-time favourite things to have (in moderation, of course). I particularly love making this in the slow cooker as it provides a steady, even heat that allows the meat to become meltingly soft and ensures the flavours mingle and develop fully. Serve this as part of a charcuterie board with lots of cornichons (or other pickles of your choice), dijon mustard and grilled bread or crusty baguette.

MAKES—2 x 375 ml jars

1 kg duck fat

1 kg boneless pork belly, skin removed, cut into 4 cm chunks

500 g boneless and rindless pork shoulder, cut into 5 cm pieces

1 onion, halved

4 garlic cloves, bruised

4 thyme sprigs, plus extra to serve

4 dried bay leaves

3 x 5 cm strips of orange zest

8 whole cloves

¼ teaspoon freshly ground white pepper

¼ teaspoon freshly grated nutmeg

¼ teaspoon ground cinnamon

1 tablespoon brandy

1½ tablespoons salt flakes

1. Preheat the oven to 150°C.
2. Place a large, flameproof casserole dish over medium heat, add the duck fat and let it melt. Add the pork belly and shoulder, onion, garlic, herbs, orange zest, spices, brandy, salt and 100 ml of water. Place a cartouche (a piece of baking paper cut to fit the dish) on top, then cover with the lid. Transfer to the middle rack of the oven and braise for 3 hours, or until the pork is soft and can be very easily shredded.
3. Let the pork cool in the dish for 1 hour, or until cool enough to handle. Using a slotted spoon, remove the pork from the fat, then shred the meat with two forks (or your hands) so it looks like floss.
4. Strain the duck fat through a fine sieve into a bowl and discard the spices, zest and herbs. Add 310 ml (1¼ cups) of the strained fat to the shredded pork and combine well; reserve the remaining fat. Taste and adjust the seasoning if necessary.
5. Firmly pack the pork rillettes into two sterilised 375 ml jars or an earthenware dish. Spoon some of the reserved duck fat over the pork rillettes to form a 5 mm thick layer (this creates a seal, ensuring the meat does not come into contact with the air, allowing it to be preserved for a couple of weeks). Scatter on the extra thyme sprigs. (Store the remaining duck fat in an airtight container in the fridge and use to roast potatoes.)
6. Cover and chill the pork rillettes in the fridge for 1–2 hours or, even better, a few days.

SLOW COOKER METHOD

Heat the slow cooker on high. Add the duck fat and let it melt. Add the pork belly and shoulder, the onion, garlic, herbs, orange zest, spices, brandy, salt and 100 ml of water. Place a cartouche (a piece of baking paper cut to fit the dish) on top, then cover with the lid. Cook on high for 3–4 hours or on low for 9–10 hours, or until the pork can be easily shredded.

Follow steps 3–6.

PULLED PORK & SLAW ROLLS

Without a doubt, this is my most crowd-pleasing dish. The best thing is it requires very little effort from the cook. A win for all! The sauce is all about using up pantry staples to create a punchy mixture that coats the shredded pork. I like to use pork scotch fillet (which is actually pork neck) because it has a perfect meat to fat ratio. You could also use shoulder, but I'd steer away from belly as I find it's too fatty for this recipe.

Pop the saucy pulled pork in the middle of the table with lots of fresh buns and homemade slaw and you will be loved – a lot – by your friends and family!

SERVES—6

1 × 1.2 kg pork scotch fillet

1 tablespoon olive oil

6 seeded milk or brioche buns

BARBECUE SAUCE

200 g good-quality barbecue sauce

1 tablespoon tomato paste

2 tablespoons dijon mustard

2 tablespoons apple cider vinegar

3 tablespoons brown sugar

2 tablespoons smoked paprika

3 garlic cloves, very finely grated

SLAW

¼ small white cabbage (about 250 g), shredded

1 carrot, julienned

½ small red onion, finely sliced

½ granny smith apple, julienned

2 tablespoons good-quality mayonnaise

1 teaspoon apple cider vinegar

salt flakes and freshly ground black pepper

1. Remove the pork from the fridge 1 hour before cooking. Preheat the oven to 150°C.
2. Combine the sauce ingredients in a jug, then mix in 500 ml (2 cups) of hot water.
3. Heat the olive oil in a flameproof casserole dish over high heat. Sear the pork all over for 8–10 minutes until browned. Pour on the sauce and turn the pork to coat. Place a cartouche (a piece of baking paper cut to fit the dish) on top, then cover with the lid. Transfer to the oven and cook for 2–2½ hours, turning halfway through, until the meat is meltingly tender.
4. Remove the pork and place on a tray. Shred the pork with two forks.
5. Place the dish back on the stovetop and reduce the sauce for 5–10 minutes until thick and glossy. Return the pulled pork to the sauce and fold through.
6. To make the slaw, combine the cabbage, carrot, onion and apple in a bowl. Mix the mayonnaise and vinegar with a pinch of salt and pepper. At the last minute, so it stays crunchy, toss the slaw with the dressing.
7. Serve the saucy pulled pork with the slaw in the buns.

SLOW COOKER METHOD

Remove the pork from the fridge 1 hour before cooking.

Combine the sauce ingredients with 125 ml (½ cup) of water. Pour into the slow cooker, add the pork and turn to coat in the sauce. Cover and cook on low for 8–9 hours until the pork is meltingly tender.

Follow step 4. If the sauce is a little watery, turn the slow cooker to high and simmer, uncovered, for 8–10 minutes until thick and glossy. Return the pulled pork to the sauce and fold through.

Follow steps 6 and 7.

SPICED GINGER BEER HAM HOCKS

Ham hocks are usually associated with pea and ham soup, but these delightful shanks are more versatile than that. When developing this recipe, I was feeling festive and decided to give the twice-cooked hocks a Christmas spin, using Chinese five spice (cinnamon, cloves, pepper, star anise and fennel seeds), orange zest and mustard. The addition of ginger beer makes them even more scrumptious, giving the meat a lovely flavour and creating a dreamy sticky glaze.

SERVES—4

2 ham hocks (around 800 g each)
750 ml (3 cups) ginger beer
3 tablespoons dark soy sauce
2 x 5 cm strips of orange zest
juice of 1 orange
3 tablespoons dijon mustard
2 tablespoons red wine vinegar
1 teaspoon Chinese five spice
soft bread rolls, butter and mustard pickles or piccalilli, to serve

1. Place the ham hocks in a stockpot and add the ginger beer, dark soy sauce and orange zest. Top with enough water to just cover the hocks. Bring to the boil, skimming off any impurities that rise to the surface. Turn the heat down to low and simmer for 1½–2 hours until the meat just starts to fall easily away from the bone, but still holds its shape.
2. Remove the ham hocks from the ginger beer stock and set aside; reserve the stock. Once the ham hocks are cool enough to handle, carefully remove and discard the skin, leaving the meat and bone intact. Place the ham hocks in a casserole or baking dish.
3. Preheat the oven to 180°C.
4. To make the glaze, pour two ladlefuls of ginger beer stock into a small saucepan and add the orange juice, mustard, vinegar and Chinese five spice. Bring to the boil, whisking regularly, and cook until thick, glossy and reduced by half.
5. Pour 250 ml (1 cup) of the reserved ginger beer stock around the ham hocks in the dish (this will keep them moist throughout the glazing process). Brush a thick coating of the glaze over the hocks and roast for 45 minutes, basting with the glaze every 10–15 minutes, until crisp and glistening.
6. I love to serve these hocks just like Christmas ham, with bread rolls, lashings of butter and mustard pickles or piccalilli.

SLOW COOKER METHOD

Place the ham hocks in the slow cooker, along with the ginger beer, dark soy sauce, orange zest and enough water to just cover. Cover with foil, then the lid and cook on high for 5–6 hours until the meat just starts to fall away from bone.

Follow steps 2–6.

STICKY TAMARIND PORK RIBS

With its distinct sweet–sour flavour, tamarind works wonders to give pork a punch of flavour. The best thing about it is you can now find tamarind at all supermarkets. This wonder ingredient combined with honey and soy sauce is all you need to make finger-licking ribs.

SERVES—4

175 g (½ cup) honey
90 g (⅓ cup) tamarind puree
80 ml (⅓ cup) soy sauce
1.5 kg American-style pork ribs
2 French shallots, finely sliced
1 lime, halved
salt flakes
45 g (½ cup) desiccated coconut, toasted
a few sprigs each of coriander and mint, to serve

1. Preheat the oven to 160°C.
2. In a bowl, combine the honey, tamarind puree, soy sauce and 250 ml (1 cup) of water.
3. Place the ribs in a single layer in a large baking dish and pour the tamarind mixture over the top. Cover the dish with a piece of baking paper, then tightly cover with two sheets of foil. Roast the ribs for 2 hours, or until the meat is almost falling away from the bones. Ideally, you want the ribs to still hold their shape so they can be easily portioned.
4. Remove the ribs from the cooking liquid and carefully transfer to a tray. Cool for 10–15 minutes.
5. Pour the cooking liquid into a large saucepan, place over medium–low heat and cook for 8–10 minutes until just starting to thicken and become slightly sticky.
6. Preheat the oven grill on high. Using a spoon or brush, baste and turn the ribs to glaze all over, then grill for 10–15 minutes, carefully turning halfway, until sticky and glistening.
7. Meanwhile, place the shallot, juice of ½ lime and a pinch of salt in a bowl, roughly stir to macerate, then stand to pickle for 5 minutes.
8. Place the ribs on a platter, sprinkle over the pickled shallot and toasted coconut and scatter on the herbs. Cut the remaining lime half into wedges and serve alongside.

SLOW COOKER METHOD

Follow step 2.

Cut the ribs in half to fit into the slow cooker; they will overlap but this is fine. Pour the tamarind mixture over the ribs. Place a cartouche (a piece of baking paper cut to fit the dish) on top, then cover with the lid. Cook on high for 4–5 hours until the meat is almost falling away from the bones.

Follow steps 4–8.

PALLARES
SOLSONA

VIETNAMESE PORK BELLY BRAISED IN COCONUT WATER

There is so much more to Vietnamese food than rice paper rolls and banh mi. Take, for instance, this home-style, slow-cooked dish of coconut-water braised pork with eggs (*thit heo kho*); it's unbelievably good as the coconut water imparts a lovely sweetness that's balanced by the saltiness of the fish sauce.

SERVES—4

1 kg boneless pork belly, skin on, cut into 3 cm pieces

2 garlic cloves, finely chopped

1 lemongrass stalk, white part only, finely chopped

1 tablespoon dark soy sauce

3 tablespoons fish sauce

1 tablespoon coconut sugar

freshly ground black pepper

1 tablespoon vegetable oil

1 red onion, chopped

3 star anise

3 tablespoons light soy sauce

1 litre coconut water

4 eggs

1 long red chilli, finely sliced on an angle

coriander leaves, to serve

steamed broccolini and rice, to serve

1. Place the pork in a large bowl. Add the garlic, lemongrass, dark soy sauce, fish sauce, coconut sugar and ½ teaspoon of pepper. Toss to coat well, cover and marinate for 3 hours or, even better, overnight.
2. Heat the vegetable oil in a large sauté pan over medium–high heat, add the onion and star anise and sauté for a few minutes to soften and lightly caramelise.
3. Add the pork and the marinade and cook, stirring regularly, for 4–5 minutes until the pork is browned on all sides. Add the light soy sauce and coconut water and bring to the boil, skimming off any impurities and fat that rise to the surface.
4. Turn the heat down to low, cover the pan with the lid and braise for 1¾–2 hours until the pork is tender.
5. Meanwhile, bring a saucepan of water to the boil, add the eggs and cook for 6 minutes. Drain and transfer to a bowl of iced water. Peel and set aside.
6. Skim off any excess fat that has risen to the surface of the sauce. Add the whole eggs, then cook for a further 5–10 minutes to allow the eggs to take on the flavour of the sauce.
7. Transfer the braised pork belly, eggs and sauce to a serving dish, scatter on the chilli and coriander leaves and serve with steamed broccolini and rice.

SLOW COOKER METHOD

Follow steps 1, 2 and 3.

Tip the pork and liquid into the slow cooker, cover and cook on low for 6 hours, or until tender.

Follow step 5.

Skim off any excess fat that has risen to the surface of the sauce. Increase the heat to high, add the eggs and cook, uncovered, for 20–30 minutes until the sauce is reduced.

Follow step 7.

STUFFED CABBAGE

This is one of my favourite ways to bring the well-suited pair of cabbage and pork together. Every culture has its own way of preparing stuffed cabbage and, yes, it's old school, but that's what I love about it. I was brought up on the French version – *chou farci* – but at the moment I really love the eastern European style, which includes caraway seeds and dill. If you don't want to reconstruct the whole cabbage, it's just as yummy when the leaves are individually stuffed with the filling and then slowly cooked in the tomato sauce.

SERVES—6

1 cabbage (about 1.8 kg), core removed with a small, sharp knife

100 g (½ cup) long-grain rice, washed 3 times in cold water

400 g pork mince

1 teaspoon caraway seeds

½ onion, finely chopped

2 garlic cloves, finely chopped

65 g finely grated parmesan

1 small handful each of dill fronds, tarragon leaves, flat-leaf parsley leaves and chervil sprigs, chopped

salt flakes and freshly ground black pepper

125 ml (½ cup) white wine (such as chardonnay)

1 litre chicken stock

1 French shallot, finely chopped

1 tablespoon capers, chopped

TIP—Use the remaining cabbage leaves for another dish, such as a stir-fry, or braise with bacon.

1. Place the cabbage in a stockpot or large, heavy-based casserole dish and half-fill with cold water. Cover with the upside-down lid (to keep the cabbage submerged) and bring to the boil. Cook over high heat for 4 minutes. Turn the cabbage, cover and cook for a further 4 minutes until slightly soft. Drain and transfer to a bowl to cool.
2. When the cabbage is cool enough to handle, carefully peel away 16 whole outer leaves, keeping them intact (see Tip).
3. To make the filling, place the rice, pork mince, caraway seeds, onion, garlic, parmesan and half the herbs in a bowl. Season with salt and pepper and mix well.
4. Place two large pieces of foil on the bench, overlapping them slightly to form a 45 cm square. Choose the four biggest cabbage leaves and arrange, overlapping with the stem end facing out, on the foil to form a circle. Add one-third of the filling and spread out, leaving a 5 cm border. Repeat this process with the next four biggest leaves and another third of the mixture, then repeat once more. Finish with a final layer of cabbage leaves.
5. To reform the cabbage, use the foil to bring the outer edge of the cabbage leaves into the centre and shape into a large round cabbage again. Press down lightly on the cabbage ball until you have the desired shape. Wrap the foil around the cabbage, leaving the base exposed.
6. Heat the stockpot or casserole dish over medium–high heat and add the wine. Bring to the boil, then add the stock.
7. Place the foil-wrapped cabbage, exposed-side down, in the stock and cover with the lid. Cook for 1½–2 hours, or until a metal skewer inserted in the centre of the cabbage feels hot when pressed to your lip.
8. Carefully remove the cabbage and place in a serving dish. Peel away the foil.
9. Bring the cooking liquid to the boil and reduce by one-third. Remove from the heat and cool slightly, then add the shallot, capers and remaining herbs. Pour over and around the cabbage, then cut into wedges to serve.

SLOW COOKER METHOD

Preheat the slow cooker to high, then add the wine.

Follow steps 1 to 5.

Once the wine is hot, add the stock. Place the foil-wrapped cabbage, exposed-side down, in the stock and cover with the lid. Turn the slow cooker to low, cover with the lid and cook for 5–6 hours, or until a metal skewer inserted in the centre of the cabbage feels hot when pressed to your lip.

Follow step 8. Turn the slow cooker to high and, when the liquid bubbles, add the shallot, capers and remaining herbs. Pour over and around the cabbage, then cut into wedges to serve.

BEEF

BEEF PHO

Pho (pronounced fur) is Vietnam's much-loved beef noodle soup. In winter, when I move down to Melbourne for half the year to film *Everyday Gourmet*, I spend a lot of time on Victoria Street in Richmond slurping comforting pho. I missed it so much when I got home, I decided to recreate my own version. It's quite easy, but you need to be patient with the long cook. The key is to get good colour on the bones and onion while they're roasting to help you achieve a deep golden broth.

Balance the pho to your taste by adjusting the fish sauce, sugar and chilli when serving.

SERVES—4

600 g fresh rice noodles or 150 g dried flat rice noodles

200 g beef eye fillet, finely sliced

1 small onion, finely sliced

270 g (3 cups) bean sprouts, rinsed

1 lemon, finely sliced

finely sliced red chilli, Thai basil leaves, coriander leaves, mint leaves and hoisin sauce, to serve

PHO BROTH

4 beef bones and/or oxtail

1 onion, quartered

1 teaspoon vegetable oil

2 star anise

1 cinnamon stick

1 teaspoon fennel seeds

1 teaspoon black peppercorns

8 cm piece of ginger, unpeeled, sliced

1 long red chilli, halved lengthways

1 x 500 g beef brisket or chuck steak, halved

1 litre beef stock

3 tablespoons fish sauce

2 tablespoons brown sugar

a squeeze of lemon juice (optional)

1. Preheat the oven to 220°C. To start on the pho broth, place the beef bones and/or oxtail and onion in a roasting tin and coat in a splash of vegetable oil. Roast for 25–35 minutes, turning halfway through to achieve a deep golden colour on the bones and onion. Add the spices and roast for a further 3–4 minutes.
2. Transfer the roasted bones, onion and spices to a stockpot, add the ginger, chilli, brisket or chuck steak, stock, fish sauce and brown sugar and pour over 1.5 litres of water to cover. Bring to the boil and skim off any impurities that rise to the surface. The impurities will continue to surface for about 20 minutes, so be sure to skim frequently.
3. Once the broth is clear of surface impurities, turn the heat down to low and cook for 3 hours. Strain and check the seasoning – it may need a little more fish sauce, sugar or a squeeze of lemon juice. Shred the brisket or chuck steak using two forks and return to the broth.
4. Blanch the fresh noodles in boiling water; or if using dried noodles, cook as per the packet instructions. Divide among four deep serving bowls. Scatter over the raw beef, onion, bean sprouts and lemon slices, then ladle over the hot pho broth. Sprinkle on the chilli and herbs and serve with the hoisin sauce alongside.

SLOW COOKER METHOD

Follow step 1.

Transfer the roasted bones, onion and spices to the slow cooker, then add the ginger, chilli, brisket or chuck steak, stock, fish sauce and brown sugar and pour over 1.5 litres of water. Cover and cook on low for 12 hours. Strain the broth and check the seasoning – it may need a little more fish sauce, sugar or a squeeze of lemon juice. Shred the brisket or chuck steak using two forks and return to the broth.

Follow step 4.

BRISKET

Brisket is one of those cuts of beef that really shines when cooked low and slow because all the connective tissue and fat melt and become gelatinous, creating the juiciest meat.

I've given my brisket a bit of a Texan feel with my spice rub, but please use this as a guide only. You can add fewer or more spices as you desire, or even change the theme entirely and give it an Asian twist by rubbing the brisket with Chinese five spice.

SERVES—6

1 x 2 kg beef brisket
1 onion, sliced
1 tablespoon olive oil
3 tablespoons tomato paste
2 tablespoons apple cider vinegar
3 tablespoons maple syrup
coleslaw (see page 117), baked potatoes with sour cream, pickles and sliced bread, to serve

SPICE RUB

2 tablespoons smoked paprika
1 tablespoon garlic powder
1 tablespoon mustard powder
1 tablespoon dried oregano
1 tablespoon freshly ground black pepper
1½ tablespoons brown sugar
1 tablespoon salt flakes

1. Combine all the spice rub ingredients in a bowl, then rub all over the beef brisket. Double wrap the brisket in plastic wrap and marinate in the fridge overnight.
2. Preheat the oven to 150°C. Scatter the onion in a large roasting tin and drizzle with the olive oil. Whisk together the tomato paste, vinegar, maple syrup and 250 ml (1 cup) of water and pour over the onion. Rest the brisket, fattier-side up, on the onion. Cover tightly with two sheets each of baking paper and foil and roast for 6–7 hours, or until the brisket is very tender.
3. Carefully remove the brisket from the tray and slice or pull apart, then place on a platter, board or tray. Spoon the onion sauce over the brisket.
4. I love to serve this style of brisket with classic accompaniments, such as coleslaw, baked potatoes with sour cream, pickles and slices of soft bread.

SLOW COOKER METHOD

Follow step 1.

Place the brisket, fattier-side up, in the slow cooker. Scatter over the onion. Whisk together the tomato paste, vinegar, maple syrup and 2 cups (500 ml) of just-boiled water and pour over the brisket and onion. Drizzle with the olive oil. Cover and cook on low for 12 hours or overnight until the brisket is very tender.

Transfer the brisket to a platter, board or tray. If the sauce is too runny, pour it into a small saucepan and boil until reduced by one-third. Slice or pull apart the brisket and spoon over the onion sauce, then follow step 4.

BEEF SHORT RIB BO SSAM

Korean *bo ssam* refers to lots of delicious bits and pieces being 'wrapped', more often than not, in lettuce leaves. The theatre of eating really comes alive with this show stopper because everyone can sit around the table and create their own *bo ssam* packages, piling each lettuce cup with lots of sticky glazed beef, rice, kimchi and herbs.

SERVES—4

4 meaty beef short ribs (about 1.4 kg)

125 ml (1/2 cup) light soy sauce

3 tablespoons caster sugar

1 litre chicken stock

1 butter lettuce, leaves separated

1 small handful each of coriander leaves and mint leaves

2 spring onions, very finely sliced

1 carrot, coarsely grated

store-bought kimchi, to serve

MARINADE

1 onion, roughly chopped

3 garlic cloves, bruised

3 cm piece of ginger, roughly chopped

3 tablespoons gochujang (Korean chilli paste) (see Note)

1 granny smith apple, cored and chopped

2 tablespoons vegetable oil

NOTE—Gochujang can be found at all Asian supermarkets.

1. Place all the marinade ingredients in a blender or small food processor and process until smooth. Transfer to a large, shallow bowl, add the ribs and turn to coat. Cover and place in the fridge to marinate for 1 hour or, for best results, overnight.
2. Preheat the oven to 170°C.
3. Place the ribs in a large, flameproof roasting tin or casserole dish in a single layer. Add the light soy sauce, sugar, stock and enough water to just cover the ribs. Bring to the boil and remove from the heat. Place a cartouche (a piece of baking paper cut to fit the dish) on top, then cover with the lid.
4. Transfer the dish to the oven to braise for 2½–3 hours until the meat just begins to pull easily away from the bone.
5. Carefully remove the ribs to a tray lined with foil. Strain the sauce into a large saucepan and place over high heat. Bring to the boil, skimming off the excess oil that comes to the surface. Reduce the heat to medium and simmer for 20–25 minutes until the sauce is sticky, thick and glossy.
6. Increase the oven temperature to 200°C. Generously brush each rib with some of the sauce and return to the oven to roast for 20 minutes, or until lightly caramelised.
7. To serve, shred the meat into the remaining sauce and serve with the lettuce cups, herbs, spring onion, carrot and kimchi.

TIP—This recipe is also great served with bao buns (found at Asian supermarkets). The buns can be steamed in the microwave.

SLOW COOKER METHOD

Follow step 1, then transfer the ribs and marinade to the slow cooker, along with the light soy sauce, sugar and stock. Cover and cook on low for 8 hours.

Follow steps 5, 6 and 7.

BEEF BOURGUIGNON

I couldn't write a slow-cooking book without including this quintessentially French dish that is so close to my heart. Beef bourguignon is, by far, the king of all beef stews and is worth making just for the beautiful smells that will fill your kitchen while it cooks. You'll notice there is only one cup of stock in my recipe yet triple the amount of wine; this ensures the sauce will be rich and deeply flavoured.

Like any slow-cooked meat dish, plan ahead and prepare this the day before serving; it will taste even better.

SERVES—4

- 750 ml (3 cups) red wine (such as cabernet sauvignon or shiraz)
- 1.5 kg chuck steak, cut into 6 cm pieces, or 1.5 kg beef cheeks, trimmed and sinew removed
- salt flakes and freshly ground black pepper
- 1 tablespoon plain flour
- 3 tablespoons olive oil
- 1 onion, quartered
- 1 large carrot, cut into 6 pieces
- 10 cm piece of celery, cut into 6 pieces
- 4 garlic cloves, bruised
- 2 tablespoons cognac or brandy
- 1 tablespoon tomato paste
- 1 bouquet garni (2 fresh or dried bay leaves and 4 thyme sprigs tied together with kitchen string), plus extra thyme leaves to serve
- 250 ml (1 cup) beef or veal stock
- 6 salad onions, trimmed and peeled
- 150 g speck or pancetta, cut into lardons
- 300 g button mushrooms, halved
- mashed potato or pappardelle, to serve

1. Preheat the oven to 160°C.
2. Pour the wine into a saucepan, bring to the boil over high heat and cook off the alcohol for 5 minutes, or until reduced by one-third. Set aside.
3. Pat the beef dry with paper towel and season with salt and pepper, then dust in the flour and shake off the excess. Heat 2 tablespoons of olive oil in a flameproof casserole dish over medium–high heat. Add the beef in batches and sear until well browned on all sides, then remove from the dish.
4. Add the vegetables and garlic to the dish and sauté for 5–8 minutes until slightly coloured. Return the beef and its juices to the dish, add the cognac or brandy and ignite with a match or lighter to flambé. Allow the flames to subside, then add the tomato paste and stir for 1 minute to coat everything in the paste. Season with salt, add the reduced wine and bring to the boil, scraping the bottom of the dish with a wooden spoon to release any caramelised bits.
5. Add the bouquet garni and stock to the dish. Place a cartouche (a piece of baking paper cut to fit the dish) on top, then cover with the lid. Place in the oven and cook for 1½–2 hours (or 2½–3 hours for beef cheeks) until the beef is very tender and the sauce has reduced by one-third.
6. Place the salad onions in a saucepan of boiling water and cook for 4–5 minutes until just tender. Drain, halve and reserve.
7. Using a slotted spoon, remove the beef and vegetables from the dish, place on a platter and cover with foil. Discard the bouquet garni.
8. Place the dish over medium heat and simmer the sauce for 8–10 minutes until it is reduced by one-third. Pour the sauce over the beef and vegetables.
9. To finish, add the remaining oil and the speck or pancetta to a frying pan. Turn the heat to medium and cook, allowing the fat to slowly render for 4–5 minutes. Once sizzling, add the salad onion and mushroom halves and cook for 3–4 minutes until golden and the speck or pancetta is crisp.
10. Scatter the speck mixture over the beef and vegetables, top with extra thyme leaves and serve with mashed potato or pappardelle.

SLOW COOKER METHOD

Follow steps 2, 3 and 4. Pour the beef and vegetable mixture into the slow cooker, add the bouquet garni and 180 ml (¾ cup) of stock. Place a cartouche (a piece of baking paper cut to fit the dish) on top, then cover with the lid. Cook on high for 4 hours or on low for 8–9 hours, or until the beef is tender.

Follow steps 6 and 7. Cook the sauce, uncovered, on high for 20–25 minutes until thickened. Pour the sauce over the beef and vegetables.

Follow steps 9 and 10.

BEEF CHEEK CHILLI

This is not your average chilli con carne made with minced meat and a packet of spice mix. This version is next-level delicious and uses beef cheeks, which are now readily available, and a tasty blend of spices. Beef cheeks are the ultimate cut of meat for slow cooking as they stay incredibly moist and gelatinous. They're also a great carrier of flavour, so are perfect for the spices I use in the sauce.

SERVES—4

2 tablespoons olive oil

3 beef cheeks (about 1 kg), sinew removed, halved

salt flakes and freshly ground black pepper

1 onion, diced

1 red capsicum, deseeded and diced

3 garlic cloves, chopped

3 coriander sprigs, stalks and roots finely chopped, leaves roughly chopped

1 tablespoon ground cumin

1 tablespoon ground coriander

1 tablespoon smoked paprika

½ teaspoon ground cinnamon

1 teaspoon dried oregano

1 chipotle chilli in adobo sauce, finely chopped, plus 2 tablespoons sauce

2 tomatoes, chopped

400 g can kidney beans, drained and rinsed

1 teaspoon red wine vinegar

plain yoghurt or sour cream, to serve

steamed brown rice, to serve

SALSA

2 corn cobs, husks and silks removed

zest and juice of 1 lime

1 long red chilli, finely chopped

a pinch of salt flakes

1. Preheat the oven to 160°C.
2. Heat half the olive oil in a flameproof casserole dish over medium–high heat. Season the beef cheeks with salt and pepper and sear for 1–2 minutes on each side until browned. Remove from the dish. Add another tablespoon of oil, then add the onion, capsicum, garlic, finely chopped coriander stalks and roots and season with salt. Turn the heat down to medium and cook, stirring regularly, for 8–10 minutes until the vegetables are softened and lightly caramelised. Add the spices and oregano and cook for a further 1 minute before adding the chipotle and adobo sauce. Stir in the tomato and cook for 5 minutes until it breaks down.
3. Return the beef cheeks to the pan and add the kidney beans and 500 ml (2 cups) of water. Place a cartouche (a piece of baking paper cut to fit the dish) on top, then cover with the lid. Transfer to the oven and braise for 2–2½ hours until the beef cheeks are tender.
4. Remove the dish from the oven and shred the beef cheeks with two forks before returning them to the sauce along with a splash of vinegar.
5. To make the salsa, preheat the oven grill. Brush the remaining oil over the corn and cook, turning regularly, for 15–20 minutes until lightly charred all over. Set aside until cool enough to handle. Alternatively, if you have a gas stove, cook directly on the gas hob, turning regularly until charred all over. Cut the kernels off the cobs and place in a bowl, then mix in the remaining salsa ingredients and the roughly chopped coriander leaves.
6. Serve the beef cheek chilli with a dollop of yoghurt or sour cream and the salsa, with steamed brown rice alongside.

SLOW COOKER METHOD

Follow step 2, then transfer the vegetable mixture to the slow cooker. Add the beef cheeks and kidney beans and 1 cup (250 ml) of water. Cover and cook on high for 5 hours or on low for 8 hours, or until the beef is tender and the sauce is thick and rich.

Follow steps 4, 5 and 6.

SLOW-COOKED BEEF STROGANOFF

Beef stroganoff, a popular mid-week family favourite, is traditionally made by quickly cooking lean meat in a creamy mushroom sauce. I adore it and thought, surely, it couldn't be improved, but it can. Slowly cooking chuck steak in worcestershire sauce and mushroom stock (from soaking dried porcini mushrooms) makes this version super special, especially when it's finished off with lots of sour cream and adorned with fresh herbs and cornichons. A famous Russian dish that dates back to the nineteenth century and has been given a bit of a revamp – now, who wouldn't love that?

SERVES—4–6

30 g dried porcini mushrooms

1 tablespoon sweet paprika, plus extra to serve

1 tablespoon plain flour

salt flakes and freshly ground black pepper

1.5 kg chuck steak, cut into 4 cm pieces

3 tablespoons olive oil

300 g button mushrooms

5 French shallots, 4 chopped and 1 finely sliced

2 garlic cloves, chopped

a splash of worcestershire sauce

120 g sour cream, plus extra to serve

reginette or pappardelle, to serve

3 dill fronds and/or flat-leaf parsley sprigs

gherkins, to serve

1. Place the dried porcini mushrooms in a bowl and cover with 500 ml (2 cups) of hot water. Let stand for 15 minutes to soften.
2. Combine the paprika, flour and a pinch of salt and pepper in a shallow bowl. Add the beef and toss to coat all over (this can also be done in a zip-lock bag as it's much easier to coat evenly). Heat half the olive oil in a large sauté pan over medium–high heat. Add the beef in batches and sear on all sides until browned, then remove from the pan.
3. Heat the remaining oil in the pan, add the button mushrooms, chopped shallot and garlic and cook over medium–high heat for 2–3 minutes until well browned.
4. Return the beef to the pan and add the worcestershire sauce, then the roughly chopped porcini mushrooms and their soaking liquid, leaving the sediment at the bottom of the bowl. Bring to the boil, season with a little more salt and turn the heat down to low. Cover with the lid and braise for 1½–2 hours until the beef is tender.
5. Stir the sour cream into the beef stroganoff and cook over medium heat for a further 5–8 minutes until a rich sauce forms. Check the seasoning; I usually like to add another splash of worcestershire sauce.
6. Serve the beef stroganoff on pasta topped with another dollop of sour cream, the dill and/or parsley and a sprinkle of extra paprika. Serve with gherkins on the side.

SLOW COOKER METHOD

Follow steps 1, 2 and 3. Place the beef and mushrooms in the slow cooker along with the worcestershire sauce, roughly chopped porcini mushrooms and 250 ml (1 cup) of their soaking liquid (leave the sediment at the bottom of the bowl). Cover and cook on high for 4–5 hours or on low for 8–9 hours, or until the beef is tender.

Add the sour cream to the beef stroganoff and cook on high for a further 10–15 minutes until the rich sauce is heated through. Check the seasoning.

Follow step 6.

OXTAIL RAGU

Oxtail (beef tail) is such an underrated cut of beef. At first, it may look like it's just pieces of fatty bone but fear not, my friends – when slow cooked for hours, the meat tucked around the knobbly bones falls away and the gelatine imparts a beautiful texture and flavour to the sauce. Forget your classic Italian ragu made with minced meat; oxtail is where the party is now.

SERVES—6

80 ml (⅓ cup) olive oil

2 kg oxtail, excess fat trimmed

salt flakes and freshly ground black pepper

1 onion, finely chopped

1 large carrot, grated

2 celery stalks, finely chopped

5 garlic cloves, chopped

a pinch of chilli flakes

2 rosemary sprigs

1 tablespoon tomato paste

250 ml (1 cup) red wine (such as shiraz or cabernet sauvignon)

2 × 400 g cans whole peeled tomatoes, crushed

250 ml (1 cup) beef or chicken stock

3 flat-leaf parsley sprigs, finely chopped, plus extra to serve

pappardelle, gnocchi (see page 52, mashed potato or polenta, to serve

1. Preheat the oven to 150°C.
2. Heat 2 tablespoons of olive oil in a large, flameproof casserole dish over medium–high heat. Season the oxtail with salt and pepper and seal on all sides for 4–5 minutes until well browned, then remove from the dish.
3. Turn the heat down to medium and heat the remaining oil in the dish. Add the vegetables, garlic, chilli flakes, rosemary and a good pinch of salt. Sauté for 10–15 minutes until softened and lightly caramelised. Scrape the bottom of the pan every now and then with a wooden spoon to ensure the vegetables don't stick. Stir in the tomato paste and cook for 1 minute, then add the wine to deglaze. Bring to the boil and cook until reduced by one-third. Add the tomatoes and stock and bring to the boil.
4. Return the oxtail and any juices on the plate to the dish and turn to coat in the sauce.
5. Place a cartouche (a piece of baking paper cut to fit the dish) on top, then cover with the lid. Braise in the oven for 3 hours, or until the meat falls easily away from the bone.
6. Remove the oxtail from the sauce and place on a chopping board. When cool enough to handle, pull the meat from the bones; discard the bones. If the sauce needs thickening, place the dish on the stovetop and simmer to reduce a little. Discard the rosemary stalks and return the meat to the sauce. Check the seasoning and fold through the parsley.
7. Serve the oxtail ragu with pappardelle, gnocchi, mashed potato or polenta.

SLOW COOKER METHOD

Follow steps 2 and 3, then pour the sauce into the slow cooker and add the oxtail and any juices on the plate. Cover and cook on low for 8 hours, or until the meat falls easily away from the bones.

Follow steps 6 and 7.

FLEMISH BEEF COBBLER

This is my idea of a perfect wintry Sunday meal – a hearty Belgian-inspired beef stew that, with the addition of dark ale, has extra depth of flavour and, if that isn't enough, is topped with a savoury, buttery, crumbly cobbler of cheesy scones. The cobbler is the perfect substitute for mash, pasta or rice and is extra special as it soaks up the lovely sauce while it cooks on top of the stew.

SERVES—6–8

- 3 tablespoons plain flour
- salt flakes and freshly ground black pepper
- 1 kg chuck steak, cut into 3 cm pieces
- 80 ml (⅓ cup) olive oil
- 2 onions, diced
- 2 carrots, chopped into 2 cm pieces
- 4 celery stalks, chopped into 2 cm pieces
- 3 garlic cloves, finely sliced
- 1 tablespoon tomato paste
- 1½ teaspoons worcestershire sauce
- 375 ml (1½ cups) dark ale or beer
- 500 ml (2 cups) beef stock
- 2 fresh or dried bay leaves
- finely chopped flat-leaf parsley, to serve (optional)

CHEESY COBBLER

- 450 g (3 cups) self-raising flour, plus extra for dusting
- 2 pinches of freshly grated nutmeg
- salt flakes
- 120 g unsalted butter, chopped and chilled
- 200 g cheddar, grated
- 360 ml buttermilk, plus 2 tablespoons extra for brushing

1. Preheat the oven to 160°C.
2. Place the flour on a plate and season with salt and pepper. Toss the chuck steak in the seasoned flour to coat, then shake off the excess.
3. Heat 2 tablespoons of olive oil in a large, flameproof casserole dish over high heat. Add the chuck steak in two batches and cook for 3–4 minutes until browned all over, then remove from the dish. Set aside.
4. Heat the remaining oil in the dish over medium–high heat. Add the onion, carrot, celery and garlic and cook, stirring frequently, for 5 minutes, or until softened. Stir in the tomato paste and worcestershire sauce and cook for a further 1 minute, or until just sticking to the bottom of the pan. Add the ale or beer and bring to the boil. Using a wooden spoon, scrape any bits from the bottom of the dish. Add the stock and bay leaves and bring to the boil.
5. Return the chuck steak to the dish.
6. Cover the dish with the lid and transfer to the oven to braise for 1¾–2 hours until the beef is tender. Remove the lid and set aside to cool for 10–15 minutes.
7. Meanwhile, for the cheesy cobbler, place the flour, nutmeg and a pinch of salt in a large bowl. Using your fingertips, rub the butter into the flour until the mixture resembles fine breadcrumbs. Add the cheese, reserving a small handful for topping, and then slowly incorporate the buttermilk until the dough is soft and a little sticky. Do not overwork the dough.
8. Tip the dough onto a lightly floured surface and shape into a disc about 3 cm thick. Cut out 11 or 12 rounds with a floured 6 cm cookie cutter, re-rolling if necessary. Place on a tray and chill until required.
9. Increase the oven temperature to 180°C.
10. Arrange the cheesy cobbler rounds on top of the stew, brush with the extra buttermilk and sprinkle over the reserved cheese. Bake for 25–30 minutes until the top is golden brown. Scatter on some parsley to serve, if desired.

SLOW COOKER METHOD

Follow steps 2, 3 and 4. Tip the vegetable mixture into the slow cooker, add the beef and stir through. Cover and cook on low for 8 hours, or until the beef is tender and the sauce is thick.

Transfer the stew to a casserole dish and continue with steps 7–10.

POT AU FEU

Pot au feu – pot roast à la Française – is the epitome of comfort food for me. It evokes many childhood memories of Sunday family lunches on cold winter days. Whether it was made in Australia by Mum or in France by my grandmother Mémé, this recipe has been prepared the same way in our family for generations. It's very French and old school, but if you know me well, you know these nostalgic dishes get me most excited about cooking and eating.

Every culture has its own version of boiled meats and broth. The French one consists not only of bone marrow (if you can't find it, don't worry, just use a few pieces of osso buco) and gravy beef, but chicken is also added to give the broth extra flavour. *Pot au feu* is served in two courses. You start with the rich bronze-coloured broth, then move on to the meltingly tender meat and sweet slow-cooked vegetables that are served with your choice of accompaniments (like mustard and cornichons). Leftovers are equally magnificent: simply shred the meat and chop the vegetables, then dress them with a mustardy vinaigrette. Bon appetit!

SERVES—4–6

- 2 beef marrow bones, halved crossways
- 1.5 kg piece of gravy beef, halved
- 2 chicken marylands
- 1 onion, peeled
- 3 carrots, peeled and halved crossways on an angle
- 2 leeks, cleaned and tied together with kitchen string
- 2 celery stalks, halved
- 2 turnips, peeled and halved
- 1 bouquet garni (2 fresh bay leaves, 3 thyme sprigs and 3 flat-leaf parsley sprigs, tied together with kitchen string)
- 3 whole cloves
- 10 black peppercorns
- 1 teaspoon rock salt
- 2 vermicelli egg noodle nests (about 60 g)
- dijon mustard, cornichons, baby pickled onions and horseradish cream, to serve

1. Place the marrow bones, beef and chicken in a stockpot and cover with plenty of cold water. Bring to the boil over high heat. Turn the heat down to medium and, using a ladle, scoop off the impurities that rise to the surface. As the broth continues to simmer, more impurities will develop, so keep skimming for 20–30 minutes until the broth is clear.
2. Meanwhile, preheat the oven grill. Place the whole onion on a baking tray and cook under the grill until mostly blackened, checking every few minutes and turning for an even colour. Alternatively, pierce the onion with a metal skewer or fork and blacken over an open flame on the stovetop. This will give the broth a lovely golden colour.
3. Add the charred onion to the broth along with the carrot, leeks, celery, turnip, bouquet garni, cloves, peppercorns and salt.
4. Gently simmer the broth for 3–4 hours until the beef is tender and the vegetables are very soft.
5. Ladle about 1 litre of strained broth into a saucepan and bring to the boil. Add the noodle nests and cook for a few minutes until al dente.
6. Divide the broth and noodles among individual bowls and serve as a start to the meal.
7. Use a slotted spoon to remove the marrow bones, beef, chicken and vegetables from the remaining broth. Cut the veggies into smaller portions and arrange on a platter with the bones and meat. Serve as the main course with the mustard, cornichons, baby pickled onions and horseradish cream.

SLOW COOKER METHOD

Follow step 2.

Place the marrow bones, beef and chicken, the charred onion, carrot, leeks, celery, turnip, bouquet garni, cloves, peppercorns and salt in the slow cooker and cover completely with water. Cover and cook on low for 5–6 hours until the meat and vegetables are tender.

Follow steps 5, 6 and 7.

SICHUAN-BRAISED BEEF NOODLES

Whenever I stop over in Hong Kong, the first thing I want is a bowl of braised beef noodles from Leaf Dessert in the central district. It may be a strange name for a noodle stand, but don't let that deter you; they make the most delicious, aromatic slow-cooked beef with homemade rice noodles and broth. The holy trinity of honey, soy sauce and Chinese cooking wine makes this bowl of happiness so addictive.

Here is my interpretation of Chinese-style braised beef noodles with a few little Jussy twists. And the best part about it is, it's so easy to make at home.

SERVES—4

1 tablespoon vegetable oil

4 beef cheeks (about 250 g each), trimmed

2 garlic cloves, chopped

4 cm piece of ginger, julienned

3 star anise

½ teaspoon sichuan peppercorns, crushed

125 ml (½ cup) shaoxing wine

3 tablespoons soy sauce

1 tablespoon Chinese black vinegar

3 tablespoons honey

8 spring onions, trimmed

800 g fresh rice noodles or 200 g dried flat rice noodles

boiling water

sesame seeds, to serve

1. Preheat the oven to 170°C.
2. Heat the vegetable oil in a large, flameproof casserole dish over medium–high heat. Add the beef and sear on both sides for 2–3 minutes until golden brown, then remove from the dish.
3. Add the garlic, ginger, star anise and sichuan pepper to the dish and cook for 2 minutes, before returning the beef along with any juices on the plate. Add the shaoxing wine and bring to the boil. Stir in the soy sauce, vinegar, honey and 375 ml (1½ cups) of water.
4. Cover the dish with the lid and transfer to the oven to braise for 2–2½ hours until the beef is meltingly tender. Add the spring onions and cook for a further 5 minutes until just tender. If the sauce needs thickening, remove the beef and bring the sauce to the boil on the stovetop for a few minutes.
5. Place the noodles in a large bowl and cover with boiling water (or prepare as per the packet instructions). Warm through for 5 minutes.
6. Portion the noodles into serving bowls and top with the beef and plenty of sauce. Scatter over the sesame seeds and serve.

SLOW COOKER METHOD

Follow steps 2 and 3.

Transfer the beef mixture to the slow cooker, cover and cook on low for 8 hours, or until the beef is tender. Add the spring onions and cook for a further 5 minutes until just tender. If the sauce needs thickening, remove the beef and simmer the sauce on high, uncovered, for 10–15 minutes.

Follow steps 5 and 6.

VEAL BLANQUETTE

This unusual French ragout is in my top five favourite dishes of all time. And like *pot au feu* (see page 144), it evokes many childhood memories. When I was sent to France to visit my grandmother, the first meal I'd always ask for was this.

Unlike many other stews and braises, veal blanquette does not sear the meat at all. In fact, the meat is gently poached in water with vegetables and herbs and the resulting aromatic veal broth is then used to make a delicious baked rice and a velouté sauce (which is where the word blanquette comes into play – the silky white sauce is blanketed over the meat). I hope you enjoy it as much as I do.

SERVES—4

1 kg veal shoulder or breast, cut into 4 cm cubes (alternatively, use 1.5 kg veal osso buco)

1 onion pierced with 3 cloves

2 celery stalks, each cut into 3 pieces

2 carrots, each cut into 3 pieces

1 leek, cleaned and tied with kitchen string

2 fresh bay leaves

2 thyme sprigs

6 black peppercorns

salt flakes

RICE

1 tablespoon extra-virgin olive oil

300 g (1½ cups) long-grain rice, washed 3 times in cold water

3 garlic cloves, bruised

1 thyme sprig

1 fresh bay leaf

salt flakes

VELOUTÉ SAUCE

30 g butter

30 g plain flour

2 tablespoons cream

juice of ¼ lemon

salt flakes and freshly ground black pepper

1 egg yolk

1. Place the veal in a stockpot and cover with plenty of cold water. Bring to a gentle boil, then reduce the heat to medium–low and, using a ladle, skim off the impurities that rise to the surface. As the broth continues to simmer, more impurities will develop, keep skimming the surface for 20–30 minutes until the broth is clear. Add the vegetables, herbs, peppercorns and a good pinch of salt and simmer for 1½–2 hours, or until the veal is meltingly tender.
2. Now start on the rice. Heat the olive oil in a heavy-based saucepan over medium–high heat and add the rice, followed by the garlic, thyme, bay leaf and a pinch of salt. Add 750 ml (3 cups) of veal broth and bring to the boil. Turn the heat down to low and cover with the lid, then cook for 15–20 minutes until the rice has completely absorbed the broth. Turn off the heat and let stand for 5 minutes.
3. To make the sauce, melt the butter in a saucepan over medium heat, add the flour and stir constantly with a wooden spoon for 1 minute to cook off the flour. Whisk in 500 ml (2 cups) of hot veal broth, a little at a time to ensure there are no lumps. Bring to the boil, stirring regularly, and cook until the sauce is thick enough to coat the back of the spoon. Turn off the heat, stir in the cream and lemon juice, then season to taste. Remove from the heat and quickly whisk in the egg yolk.
4. Using a slotted spoon, remove the veal and vegetables from the broth and place in a large, shallow serving dish. Strain the remaining stock, portion into containers and freeze for another use (like sauces, risottos and soups). Pour the sauce over the top and serve with the fragrant rice.

SLOW COOKER METHOD

Place the veal, vegetables, herbs, peppercorns and a good pinch of salt in the slow cooker. Pour in enough water to completely cover the veal and vegetables by at least 4 cm. Cover and cook on high for 5–6 hours or on low for 8–10 hours, or until the veal is meltingly tender.

Follow steps 2, 3 and 4.

LAMB

BRAISED LAMB CHOPS WITH GRAPES

Slow cooking is not restricted to large secondary cuts of meat, it also works nicely with a fattier style of chop. Here, I give lamb forequarter chops an agrodolce (sweet and sour) feel by adding grapes and vinegar, which helps cut through the fat. I love the addition of allspice as it imparts a lovely pungent flavour and works so well with lamb. You can replace the allspice with ground cumin, ground coriander or even smoked paprika for something different.

SERVES—4

1 teaspoon olive oil

4 lamb forequarter chops (about 850 g)

1 teaspoon ground allspice

salt flakes and freshly ground black pepper

2 red onions, each cut into 8 wedges

2 garlic cloves, chopped

3 Swiss chard or silverbeet leaves, stalks finely chopped, leaves chopped

2 preserved lemon wedges, flesh discarded and skin finely sliced

1½ tablespoons red wine vinegar

500 ml (2 cups) chicken stock

200 g (about 1 cup) seedless red grapes

1. Preheat the oven to 160°C.
2. Heat the olive oil in a large, flameproof casserole dish over medium–high heat. Add the lamb and sear for 2 minutes on each side until browned. Season with the allspice, salt and pepper, then remove from the dish.
3. Add the onion to the dish and cook, stirring occasionally, for a few minutes to caramelise. Add the garlic and cook for 30 seconds, then stir in the chopped Swiss chard or silverbeet stalks. Cook for 2–3 minutes to soften, then add the chopped Swiss chard or silverbeet leaves, preserved lemon, vinegar and a pinch of salt and cook, stirring occasionally, for a few minutes. Pour in the stock and bring to the boil.
4. Return the lamb to the dish and cover with the lid, leaving it slightly ajar. Transfer to the oven and braise for 40–45 minutes until the lamb is tender.
5. Using a slotted spoon, remove the lamb and most of the vegetables from the dish. Arrange on a platter and set aside, keeping warm. Skim off any excess fat that has formed on the surface of the sauce.
6. Place the dish over medium–high heat and bring the sauce to the boil. Add the grapes and cook for 5–8 minutes until softened and warmed through and the sauce is reduced.
7. Pour the grapes and sauce over the lamb and vegetables and serve.

SLOW COOKER METHOD

Follow steps 2 and 3.

Add the vegetables, stock and seared lamb chops to the slow cooker and cover with the lid. Cook on high for 3 hours or on low for 5–6 hours, or until the lamb is tender.

Follow step 5. Turn the slow cooker to high and cook, uncovered, until the sauce comes to the boil. Add the grapes and cook for 15 minutes until the grapes are warmed through and the sauce is reduced. Pour over the lamb and vegetables and serve.

DUKKAH-CRUSTED LAMB RIBS

'Finger-licking good' is the comment I get when I make these ribs for my friends. Lamb ribs may not be as common as pork ribs but they really should be because they're totally delectable. The best part about this inexpensive cut of lamb is it's super easy to achieve meltingly tender meat that pulls away easily from the bone. I've given my lamb ribs an Egyptian feel by coating them in a pomegranate molasses glaze and then dunking them in homemade dukkah to create a lovely crust. I suggest making a double batch of dukkah and storing it in an airtight container in the cupboard as I think these are going to be a regular on your menu, just like they are for me.

SERVES—6

170 ml (2/3 cup) pomegranate molasses

2 tablespoons brown sugar

250 ml (1 cup) beef stock

salt flakes

2 kg lamb ribs

mint leaves, to serve

1/2 pomegranate, seeds removed

lemon wedges, to serve

DUKKAH

1 tablespoon blanched almonds

1 tablespoon sesame seeds

1 tablespoon coriander seeds

1 tablespoon cumin seeds

2 teaspoons fennel seeds

1/2 teaspoon black peppercorns

1/2 teaspoon salt flakes

DRESSING

3 tablespoons tahini

juice of 1/2 lemon

1/2 garlic clove, finely chopped

salt flakes and freshly ground black pepper

1. Place all the dukkah ingredients in a small food processor and process until a fine crumb forms.
2. Preheat the oven to 160°C.
3. Whisk together the pomegranate molasses, sugar, stock and a good pinch of salt. Toss the ribs in the marinade.
4. Place the ribs, side by side, in a single layer in a large roasting tin. It's okay if the ribs are touching. Pour the remaining pomegranate molasses mixture over the ribs.
5. Cover the tin tightly with two pieces of foil. Roast for 1½–2 hours until the lamb is tender but not completely falling off the bone. Remove the lamb from the oven.
6. Line two large trays with foil, then baking paper (this will save time when washing up later!). Remove the ribs from the cooking liquid and arrange on the prepared trays.
7. Increase the oven temperature to 200°C.
8. Pour the sauce into a small saucepan. Using a spoon, skim the excess fat from the sauce, then cook over high heat for 10–12 minutes, or until reduced by two-thirds and sticky and glossy.
9. Brush each rib with the sticky glaze. Sprinkle over the dukkah and roast for 10–15 minutes to toast the dukkah crust and allow the lamb to become crispy.
10. Place the dressing ingredients in a bowl, add 3 tablespoons of water and mix well. Season to taste.
11. Transfer the lamb ribs to a platter, scatter over the mint and pomegranate seeds and serve with the dressing alongside for dipping and lemon wedges for squeezing.

SLOW COOKER METHOD

Follow steps 1 and 3.

Place the ribs in the slow cooker; it's okay if they overlap. Pour the remaining pomegranate molasses over each rib. Cover and cook, turning the ribs halfway through, on high for 4 hours or on low for 8 hours, or until tender.

Follow step 6 and preheat the oven to 200°C.

Follow steps 8–11.

LANCASHIRE HOTPOT

Full of deep, rich flavours from not one but three different cuts of lamb, this quintessential English favourite is perfect for feeding a hungry crowd in winter. The last time I had this hotpot was in a quaint country pub in England. They served it with pickled cabbage, which I thought was a fabulous idea as it provided a welcome hit of acidity and crunch to this hearty dish.

SERVES—6

1 teaspoon olive oil, plus extra for greasing

1 kg boned lamb shoulder, trimmed and cut into 4 cm pieces

500 g lamb loin chops, fat trimmed

salt flakes and freshly ground black pepper

3 lamb sausages

3 large onions, sliced

4 thyme sprigs, leaves picked and finely chopped, plus extra leaves to serve

6 fresh bay leaves

2 tablespoons plain flour

3 tablespoons worcestershire sauce

375 ml (1½ cups) chicken stock

1.2 kg desiree potatoes, peeled and sliced into 5 mm thick rounds

25 g butter, chopped

QUICK PICKLED CABBAGE

¼ red cabbage, finely sliced

125 ml (½ cup) apple cider vinegar

2 teaspoons brown sugar

1 teaspoon salt flakes

1. Heat the olive oil in a large frying pan over medium–high heat. Season the lamb shoulder and chops with salt and pepper. Add the shoulder, chops and sausages in two batches to the pan. Sear, turning constantly, for 5 minutes, or until browned all over, then transfer to a plate. Chop the sausages into thirds. Add the onion, thyme and bay leaves to the pan and cook in the residual oil, stirring frequently, for 3–4 minutes until softened. Stir in the flour and cook for 1 minute, or until sticking to the bottom of the pan. Add the worcestershire sauce and stock, bring to the boil and cook for 4 minutes, or until slightly reduced. Remove from the heat and stand until required.
2. Preheat the oven to 150°C and grease a 5 litre casserole dish with extra olive oil. Arrange one-third of the potato, in a single layer and overlapping slightly, in the base of the dish. Next, top with half the onion mixture, then half the mixed seared meat. Repeat this process, finishing with a layer of slightly overlapping potato slices. Scatter over the butter and cover with the lid. Bake for 3½ hours, or until the meat is tender.
3. While the hotpot is cooking, make the quick pickled cabbage. Place the cabbage in a heatproof bowl. Combine the vinegar, sugar, salt and 125 ml (½ cup) of water in a small saucepan and bring to the boil. Pour over the cabbage, cover and place in the fridge to chill until required.
4. Increase the oven temperature to 210°C and remove the lid from the casserole. Scatter over the extra thyme and cook for a further 30–35 minutes until the potato on top is golden. Serve with the pickled cabbage.

SLOW COOKER METHOD

Follow step 1. Brush a little olive oil over the base of the slow cooker.

Arrange one-third of the potato in a single layer in the slow cooker. Next, top with half the onion mixture, then add half the mixed seared meat. Repeat this process, finishing with a layer of slightly overlapping potato slices. Scatter over the butter and extra thyme and cover. Cook on low for 8 hours, or until the potato is cooked through and the meat is tender.

Follow step 3, then follow step 4 by transferring the uncovered slow cooker bowl to the oven. Serve the hotpot as is with the pickled cabbage.

GREEK LAMB & RISONI STEW

I first made this stew on my TV show *Everyday Gourmet,* and it was so popular I just had to include it in this book. My original recipe used lamb shanks, but I really wanted to show off the under-utilised lamb neck as it's economical, cooks in the same amount of time and the braised meat is unbelievably tender. I've given my lamb neck stew a Greek twist (quite similar to an old-fashioned *youvetsi*) by adding lots of garlic, oregano, cinnamon and some feta and al dente risoni. Serve with a side of steamed silverbeet or broccoli or try folding through some peas and/or spinach just before adding the risoni.

SERVES—4

1 x 1.5 kg boneless lamb neck, cut into 4 pieces

salt flakes and freshly ground black pepper

2 tablespoons extra-virgin olive oil, plus extra for splashing

1 onion, chopped

4 garlic cloves, chopped

1 teaspoon dried oregano

1 cinnamon stick

1 tablespoon tomato paste

400 g can whole peeled tomatoes, crushed

500 ml (2 cups) chicken stock

330 g (1½ cups) dried risoni pasta

50 g feta, crumbled

grilled pita breads, to serve (optional)

1. Preheat the oven to 160°C.
2. Season the lamb with salt and pepper. Heat the olive oil in a large, flameproof casserole dish over high heat. Add the lamb and sear on all sides until browned, then remove from the dish. Add the onion and garlic to the dish and cook for 3–4 minutes until softened. Stir in the oregano, cinnamon and tomato paste and cook for a further 1 minute.
3. Return the lamb to the dish and add the tomatoes, stock and a pinch of salt and pepper. Cover and transfer to the oven to braise for 2–2½ hours until the lamb is soft and pulls apart easily with two forks.
4. Remove the lamb from the sauce and shred into chunks. If the sauce is a little thin, place the dish over medium heat and reduce for a few minutes to thicken. Return the chunks of lamb to the sauce.
5. Bring a large saucepan of salted water to the boil. Add the risoni and cook until just al dente. Drain and mix through a splash of oil.
6. Add the risoni to the lamb stew and fold through. Place on a platter, sprinkle over the feta and serve with grilled pita breads, if desired.

NOTE—A great substitute for lamb neck is four French-trimmed lamb shanks (about 300 g each).

SLOW COOKER METHOD

Follow step 2.

Place the vegetables and lamb in the slow cooker and add the tomatoes, stock and a pinch of salt and pepper. Cover and cook on low for 8 hours, or until the lamb is soft and pulls apart easily with two forks. Remove the lamb from the sauce and shred into chunks. If the sauce is too thin, turn the slow cooker up to high and reduce for 8–10 minutes. Return the chunks of lamb to the sauce.

Follow steps 5 and 6.

LAMB & SPINACH CURRY WITH QUICK NAAN

Please don't be deterred by the long list of ingredients; most are spices you'll already have in your pantry. Making your own spice paste creates a far more authentic and tasty Indian curry and, because lamb is such a great carrier of flavour, I've been quite liberal with my blend. I like to use lamb shoulder here because it has so much connective tissue that helps enrich the sauce during the low and slow cook. To freshen the whole curry up, I love the addition of spinach. Oh, and don't forget the quick naan. You can adorn yours with pickles, keep it plain like I have here, or why not add crushed garlic or crumbled cheese to really show off?

SERVES—4–6

3 tablespoons melted ghee or olive oil

2 curry leaf sprigs

1 kg boned lamb shoulder, trimmed and diced

3 onions, sliced

1 teaspoon brown mustard seeds

4 garlic cloves, finely chopped

3 cm piece of ginger, finely grated

1 long green chilli, finely chopped, plus extra to serve

1 tablespoon brown sugar

2 teaspoons ground coriander

2 teaspoons ground turmeric

1 teaspoon ground cumin

1 teaspoon sweet paprika

250 g (1 cup) plain yoghurt, plus extra to serve (optional)

1 teaspoon garam masala

280 g baby spinach leaves

steamed basmati rice, to serve

lime pickles and/or mango chutney, to serve

QUICK NAAN

225 g (1½ cups) self-raising flour, plus extra for dusting

340 g (1⅓ cups) plain yoghurt

2 tablespoons melted ghee

salt flakes

1. Heat the ghee or olive oil in a large sauté pan over medium heat. Add the curry leaves and cook for 1–2 minutes until crisp. Drain on paper towel and reserve. Add the lamb in batches and cook, turning, for 5–8 minutes until slightly browned. Transfer to a plate. Next, add the onion and mustard seeds to the pan and cook, stirring frequently, over medium heat for 5–8 minutes until the onion is softened and turning golden brown. Return the lamb to the dish.
2. Combine the garlic, ginger, chilli, sugar, coriander, turmeric, cumin, paprika and 3 tablespoons of water in a bowl and mix to form a paste. Add the paste to the onion and lamb and cook, stirring to coat everything in the spices, for 3–4 minutes until fragrant and slightly darkened. Add the yoghurt and mix through.
3. Bring the curry to the boil, then turn the heat down to low. Cover and cook for 1½–2 hours until the lamb is tender. Check halfway through; if the curry is a little dry, simply add 3 tablespoons of water.
4. Stir the garam masala and spinach into the curry and cook for a further 3–4 minutes to wilt the spinach.
5. To make the quick naan, place the flour in a bowl. Make a well in the centre, add the yoghurt and incorporate into the flour until a smooth dough forms. Divide into four to six portions and press out into 10 cm ovals. Brush the ghee over the top of each naan and season with salt. Heat a non-stick frying pan or chargrill pan over high heat. Add one naan and cook, ghee-side down, for 2 minutes, or until golden. Flip, reduce the heat to medium–low and cook for a further 3 minutes, or until cooked through. Transfer to a plate and cover with foil, then repeat with the remaining naan.
6. Scatter the crispy curry leaves and extra chilli over the curry and serve with the naan bread, steamed basmati rice, extra yoghurt and classic condiments of your choice, such as lime pickles and/or mango chutney.

SLOW COOKER METHOD

Follow steps 1 and 2.

Place the curry in the slow cooker, cover and cook on high for 3½–4 hours or on low for 8 hours, or until the lamb is tender.

Add the garam masala and spinach to the curry and cook for a further 15–20 minutes to wilt the spinach.

Follow steps 5 and 6.

CHINESE-STYLE LAMB MEATBALLS

Meatballs should not be pigeonholed as Italian cuisine; in fact, there's the famous Chinese rendition called lion's head (the name comes from the giant size of the meatball in the original recipe). Usually made with pork mince and water chestnuts, I've made mine with lamb – and the results are fantastic. There's a sort of Mongolian lamb vibe happening with lots of sticky, sweet and salty flavours created by adding soy sauce and sugar to the sauce. I think these meatballs are going to be one of your new mid-week favourites.

SERVES—4

3 tablespoons vegetable oil
2 small onions, thickly sliced
3 cm piece of ginger, grated
3 garlic cloves, chopped
1 star anise
125 ml (½ cup) shaoxing wine
3 tablespoons brown sugar
3 tablespoons tamarind puree
125 ml (½ cup) light soy sauce
500 ml (2 cups) chicken stock
1 tablespoon cornflour, mixed with 2 tablespoons water
1 tablespoon sesame seeds
2 spring onions, finely sliced
steamed greens and rice or rice noodles, to serve

MEATBALLS

750 g lamb mince
35 g (⅓ cup) panko breadcrumbs
2 tablespoons hoisin sauce
2 teaspoons Chinese five spice
2 spring onions, finely chopped

1. Heat 2 tablespoons of vegetable oil in a large sauté pan over medium–high heat. Add the onion and sauté for 3 minutes, or until golden. Add the ginger, garlic and star anise and cook for a further 2 minutes, or until aromatic. Pour in the shaoxing wine and bring to the boil. Stir in the brown sugar, tamarind puree, light soy sauce and stock. Bring to the boil, then turn the heat down to medium–low and simmer for 15–20 minutes until the sauce is reduced by one-third.
2. Combine all the meatball ingredients in a large bowl and mix thoroughly with your hands. Divide the mixture into eight portions. Wet your hands and shape the mixture into balls. Heat the remaining oil in a large, heavy-based frying pan over medium–high heat and fry the meatballs in two batches, shaking the pan and turning them regularly, for 5–6 minutes until browned all over.
3. Transfer the meatballs to the sauce and gently turn to coat without breaking them. Cover, leaving the lid slightly ajar, and cook over low heat for 35–40 minutes until the meatballs are cooked through. Remove the meatballs from the pan. Increase the heat to medium and whisk in the cornflour paste. Cook for a few minutes until the sauce is thick and glossy. Return the meatballs to the pan.
4. Scatter the sesame seeds and spring onion over the meatballs and serve with steamed greens and rice or rice noodles.

SLOW COOKER METHOD

Follow steps 1 and 2.

Transfer the sauce and meatballs to the slow cooker. Cover and cook on high for 2 hours or on low for 4 hours.

Remove the meatballs and turn the slow cooker up to high. Add the cornflour mixture and cook for 5–8 minutes to thicken, then return the meatballs to the cooker.

Follow step 4.

ZA'ATAR LAMB SHOULDER

There are no tricks when it comes to cooking meltingly tender, pull-apart lamb shoulder. Once it's in the oven or slow cooker, the lamb requires very little attention and simply needs low-temperature cooking for a lengthy period of time. When I'm organised, I love to slow cook the shoulder a day or two ahead and chill it. The next day, I scrape off the film of fat, bring the lamb to room temperature, then reheat it at 200°C for 30 minutes. This tip is great for a dinner party. You'll have more control in the kitchen as the main job is done and dusted, and the lamb will taste even better as the aromatic za'atar has had more time to mingle with the meat.

SERVES—4

1 x 1.5 kg lamb shoulder, bone in and shank detached

1 onion, peeled and cut into 8 wedges

800 ml chicken stock

2 very ripe tomatoes

salt flakes

LABNE

500 g Greek yoghurt

ZA'ATAR SPICE MIX

2 tablespoons dried oregano

2 tablespoons thyme leaves

1 teaspoon dried mint

3 tablespoons sumac

3 tablespoons sesame seeds

3 tablespoons olive oil, plus extra for drizzling

salt flakes and freshly ground black pepper

TO SERVE

flat-leaf parsley leaves

mint leaves

finely sliced red onion

flatbreads

lemon wedges

1. For the labne, place a sieve lined with two clean Chux cloths or a piece of muslin over a bowl and add the yoghurt. Bring the sides of the cloth together and twist, then tie with a rubber band to secure. Refrigerate for 5 hours or, even better, overnight to drain and release as much liquid (whey) as possible. Discard the whey.
2. Take the lamb out of the fridge at least 1 hour before cooking.
3. Place all the za'atar spice mix ingredients in a small food processor (or use a mortar and pestle) and process or pound to a crumb-like consistency. Taste and season generously with more salt and pepper if needed. Set 2 tablespoons aside.
4. Preheat the oven to 160°C. Rub the za'atar spice mix all over the lamb, adding most to the top.
5. Place the onion wedges in a large, deep baking dish and rest the lamb and shank on top. Pour the stock around the lamb. Cover the dish tightly with two layers of foil and roast for 3–3½ hours until the meat pulls easily away from the bone.
6. Increase the oven temperature to 200°C. Remove the foil and return the lamb to the oven.
7. Roast the lamb for a further 30 minutes to crisp up the skin and toast the spice crust.
8. Cut the tomatoes in half, then squeeze out and discard the seeds. Using a box grater, grate the tomato flesh, discarding the skins. Place the tomato in a bowl and add a pinch of salt.
9. Spread the labne over a platter, spoon over the tomato and drizzle with extra oil. Place the lamb on top and spoon around some of the cooking juices. Scatter over the fresh herbs and red onion, then sprinkle on the reserved za'atar spice mix. Serve with flatbreads of your choice and lemon wedges on the side.

SLOW COOKER METHOD

Follow steps 1, 2 and 3.

Rub a crust of za'atar spice mix all over the lamb, adding most to the top. Place the onion wedges and stock in the slow cooker and rest the lamb shoulder and shank on top. Cover and cook on low for 9–9½ hours until the meat pulls easily away from the bone.

Preheat the oven to 200°C. Carefully remove the lamb from the slow cooker and place on a baking tray. Follow steps 7, 8 and 9.

LAMB SHANK PIES

What's not to love about saucy, red wine–braised lamb shanks crowned with flaky, buttery puff pastry?

I make this when I want to wow my guest as there is something so theatrical about an exposed shank piercing a golden pastry top. What I love most about these pies is that the pastry is cooked separately so it's crispy on both sides. If you're super organised, make the shanks a day ahead and gently reheat the following day while you bake the pastry.

If you want to change it up, this stew is also delicious served with mash or pappardelle, or fold the shredded meat through gnocchi (see page 52). Cue drooling.

SERVES—4

- 4 lamb shanks, French trimmed
- salt flakes and freshly ground black pepper
- 1 tablespoon olive oil
- 1 onion, diced
- 1 carrot, diced
- 1 celery stalk, diced
- 300 g button mushrooms, quartered
- 2 garlic cloves, chopped
- 1 rosemary sprig
- 1 star anise
- 1 tablespoon tomato paste
- 500 ml (2 cups) red wine (such as shiraz or cabernet sauvignon)
- 1 litre beef stock
- 375 g good-quality butter puff pastry, rolled out to 3 mm thick
- 1 egg, whisked
- 3 flat-leaf parsley sprigs, chopped

1. Preheat the oven to 160°C. Season the shanks with salt and pepper.
2. Heat half the olive oil in a large, flameproof casserole dish over high heat. Sear the lamb shanks on all sides for 5–6 minutes, then remove from the dish and place on a plate. Add the remaining oil and sauté the onion, carrot and celery for a few minutes until softened and golden. Add the mushroom, garlic, rosemary and star anise. Stir in the tomato paste and cook for a further 30 seconds, then add the wine and boil for 3–5 minutes until almost evaporated. Pour in the stock and again bring to the boil. Return the lamb shanks to the dish.
3. Place a cartouche (a piece of baking paper cut to fit the dish) on top, then cover with the lid. Transfer to the oven to braise for 2 hours, or until the lamb is soft and pulls easily away from the bone.
4. While the lamb shanks are cooking, cut out four pastry rounds using the rim of your chosen pie dishes as a guide (my dishes are 11 cm in diameter). Place the pastry rounds on a baking tray lined with baking paper. Using a 3 cm diameter cookie cutter, cut out and discard the centre from each round (the pastry will be a doughnut shape). Lightly brush with the whisked egg and chill, uncovered, until ready to bake.
5. Increase the oven temperature to 200°C. Bake the pastry rounds for 15–20 minutes, or until puffed and golden.
6. Remove the lamb shanks from the sauce and shred the meat, reserving the bones for presentation. Reduce the sauce over medium heat for 8–10 minutes, or until rich and reduced by one-third. Fold the meat through the sauce and add the parsley.
7. Place the bone in the centre of each pie dish and spoon in the meat sauce. Top with the pastry, allowing the bone to poke through the central hole.

SLOW COOKER METHOD

Follow steps 1 and 2. Place the lamb shanks and sauce in the slow cooker. Place a cartouche (a piece of baking paper cut to fit the dish) on top, then cover with the lid and cook on low for 8–10 hours, or until the meat falls easily away from the bone.

Preheat the oven to 200°C. Follow step 4. Bake the pastry rounds for 15–20 minutes, or until puffed and golden.

Follow steps 6 and 7.

LAMB NAVARIN

This beautifully simple way of gently braising lamb and vegetables in white wine shows off the comforting allure of French cooking. I love to make this when winter just turns into spring, when lamb is extra juicy and all the new-season vegetables start to sprout up.

SERVES—4–6

1 tablespoon olive oil

1 × 1.2 kg boned lamb shoulder, trimmed and cut into 4 cm pieces

salt flakes and freshly ground black pepper

1 tablespoon plain flour

1 teaspoon tomato paste

1 large carrot, cut into 3 cm thick rounds

½ small celeriac, cut into 3 cm cubes

3 garlic cloves, chopped

1 bouquet garni (2 fresh bay leaves, 1 rosemary sprig and 1 flat-leaf parsley sprig tied together with kitchen string)

250 ml (1 cup) white wine (such as chardonnay)

250 ml (1 cup) chicken stock

8 small kipfler potatoes, peeled

8 small pickling onions, peeled and halved

8 asparagus spears, woody ends trimmed

65 g (½ cup) frozen baby peas

chopped flat-leaf parsley leaves, to serve

1. Heat the olive oil in a large sauté pan over medium–high heat. Season the lamb all over with salt and pepper and seal on all sides for 5–6 minutes until lightly golden. Sprinkle in the flour, stir and cook for 1 minute, ensuring each piece of lamb is coated. Now stir in the tomato paste, carrot, celeriac, garlic and bouquet garni. Season with salt.
2. Pour the wine into the pan, bring to the boil and cook for 4–5 minutes until reduced by one-third. Stir in the stock.
3. Place a cartouche (a piece of baking paper cut to fit the pan) on top, then cover with the lid. Cook over low heat for 1½ hours, stirring halfway through.
4. Add the potatoes and onion halves to the stew and nestle into the sauce. Cook for a further 30 minutes, or until the potatoes and onion halves are cooked through and the lamb is tender.
5. If you'd like to thicken the sauce a little, use a slotted spoon to remove the lamb and vegetables. Bring the sauce to the boil and cook for 5 minutes. Return the lamb and vegetables to the sauce.
6. Bring a saucepan of salted water to the boil. Add the asparagus and peas. When the water has come back to the boil (about 1 minute), drain the blanched vegetables. Scatter the peas and parsley over the lamb navarin and serve with the asparagus.

SLOW COOKER METHOD

Follow steps 1 and 2. Transfer the lamb and vegetables to the slow cooker, place a cartouche (a piece of baking paper cut to fit the dish) on top, then cover with the lid. Cook on low for 8 hours, or until the lamb is tender. Turn the slow cooker up to high and add the potatoes and onion halves, then cover and cook for a further 1 hour, or until the potatoes and onion halves are cooked through and the lamb is tender.

Using a slotted spoon, remove the lamb and vegetables. Simmer the sauce on high for a further 30 minutes to thicken a little. Return the lamb and vegetables to the sauce.

Follow step 6.

LAMB BIRYANI

Biryani is one of those dishes I never order in a restaurant as there is something so homely about it. In actual fact, I first fell in love with it when my friends Nishath and Faiz cooked it for me. Their authentic biryani was magnificent, with layer upon layer of fragrant lamb curry and fluffy rice – definitely a labour of love.

I've simplified my version a bit by adding the par-boiled rice to the top of the curry. Be sure to cover the rice not only with the lid but also with foil so the rice steams and stays moist throughout the second cook. This also goes for the slow cooker.

SERVES—4–6

2 tablespoons olive oil

2 small onions, finely sliced

1 cinnamon stick

2 teaspoons cumin seeds

5 cardamom pods, bruised

5 whole cloves

2 tomatoes, quartered

juice of 1 lemon

400 g (2 cups) basmati rice, washed 3 times in cold water

3 fresh bay leaves

3 tablespoons milk

a pinch of saffron threads

30 g butter

toasted flaked almonds, mint leaves and chutney, to serve

MARINATED LAMB

800 g boned lamb shoulder, trimmed and diced

3 cm piece of ginger, finely grated

5 garlic cloves, finely grated

185 g (¾ cup) Greek yoghurt

2 teaspoons ground coriander

2 teaspoons garam masala

1 teaspoon mild chilli powder (I use kashmiri)

½ teaspoon freshly grated nutmeg

1 teaspoon salt flakes

1. Combine all the marinated lamb ingredients in a large bowl. Cover and refrigerate overnight.
2. Heat the olive oil in a large, flameproof casserole dish over medium–high heat. Add the onion and sauté for 3–4 minutes to soften. Stir in the whole spices and cook for a further 1 minute, or until aromatic. Add the lamb and marinade and cook, stirring regularly, for 8 minutes, or until the lamb is lightly browned.
3. Add the tomato and 375 ml (1½ cups) of water and bring to the boil. Reduce the heat to low, cover and cook for 1½–2 hours until the lamb is tender. Stir through the lemon juice. In the last 15 minutes of cooking, preheat the oven to 180°C.
4. Bring a saucepan of water to the boil. Add the rice and bay leaves and cook for 2–3 minutes to par-cook the rice. Drain.
5. Place the milk, saffron and butter in a small saucepan and bring to the boil. Remove from the heat.
6. Remove half of the lamb from the dish and reserve. Spoon half the par-cooked rice over the lamb stew in the dish and spread out evenly. Spoon over the reserved lamb and top with the remaining rice. Drizzle over the milk mixture. Cover tightly with foil, then with the lid and cook in the oven for 25–30 minutes.
7. Scatter the flaked almonds and mint leaves over the biryani and serve with chutney on the side.

SLOW COOKER METHOD

Follow steps 1 and 2, then transfer the lamb mixture to the slow cooker. Add the tomato and water, cover and cook on high for 4 hours or on low for 7–8 hours, or until the lamb is really tender. Stir through the lemon juice.

Follow steps 4, 5 and 6, then cover and cook in the slow cooker on high for 45–60 minutes until the rice is cooked through.

Follow step 7.

STUFFED LEG OF LAMB

A stuffing made up of garlic, anchovies, rosemary and lemon takes your standard roast leg of lamb to the next level. Anchovies and lamb are actually a very common pairing in French and Italian cooking, so don't be deterred – I assure you the anchovies don't give the roast a fishy flavour; rather they impart a salty, savoury note. I highly recommend asking your butcher to debone the lamb leg as it'll make life much easier for you. If you have a meat thermometer, probe the meat once the cooking time ends. The perfect internal temperature should be stabilised at 65–70°C.

SERVES—4

1 × 1.6 kg boned leg of lamb, sinew and excess fat removed

salt flakes and freshly ground black pepper

1 tablespoon olive oil

3 onions, finely sliced

125 ml (½ cup) white wine (such as chardonnay)

250 ml (1 cup) chicken stock

steamed seasonal greens, to serve

STUFFING

3 garlic cloves, chopped

salt flakes

3 anchovy fillets in oil, drained

2 rosemary sprigs, leaves picked and finely chopped, plus extra leaves to serve

zest of 1 lemon

½ teaspoon chilli flakes

2 tablespoons dijon mustard

120 g (1½ cups) fresh breadcrumbs

3 tablespoons olive oil

1. Take the lamb out of the fridge 1 hour before cooking. Preheat the oven to 200°C.
2. For the stuffing, pound the garlic and a good pinch of salt to a paste using a mortar and pestle. Add the anchovy, rosemary, lemon zest and chilli flakes and pound again to form a rough paste, then mix in the mustard. (If you don't have a mortar and pestle, just finely chop everything together.) Transfer to a bowl, add the breadcrumbs and olive oil and mix to combine.
3. Season the lamb with salt and pepper, then place, fat-side down, on a chopping board. Spread the stuffing evenly over the lamb, then roll up to enclose the stuffing and secure with kitchen string, tying firmly at 2 cm intervals.
4. Heat the olive oil in a large, flameproof casserole dish over high heat. Add the stuffed lamb and cook, turning, for 6–8 minutes until golden brown on all sides. Add the onion and cook for a further 3 minutes, or until softened. Deglaze with the wine and pour in the stock.
5. Transfer the dish to the oven and braise, uncovered, for 25 minutes. Reduce the oven temperature to 160°C and cover with the lid. Braise for a further 40–50 minutes until the lamb is tender.
6. Remove the stuffed lamb from the sauce, place on a plate and rest, loosely covered with foil, for 15–20 minutes.
7. Carve the stuffed lamb, arrange on a platter and spoon over the braising juices and onion. Scatter with extra rosemary leaves and serve with your choice of steamed greens.

SLOW COOKER METHOD

Take the lamb out of the fridge 1 hour before cooking.

Follow steps 2, 3 and 4, then tip the liquid and onion into the slow cooker. Place the stuffed lamb on top, cover and cook on low for 8 hours, turning the lamb halfway through.

Follow step 6, then transfer the sauce to a saucepan and place over high heat. Bring to the boil and cook for 15 minutes, or until reduced by half.

Follow step 7.

DESSERT

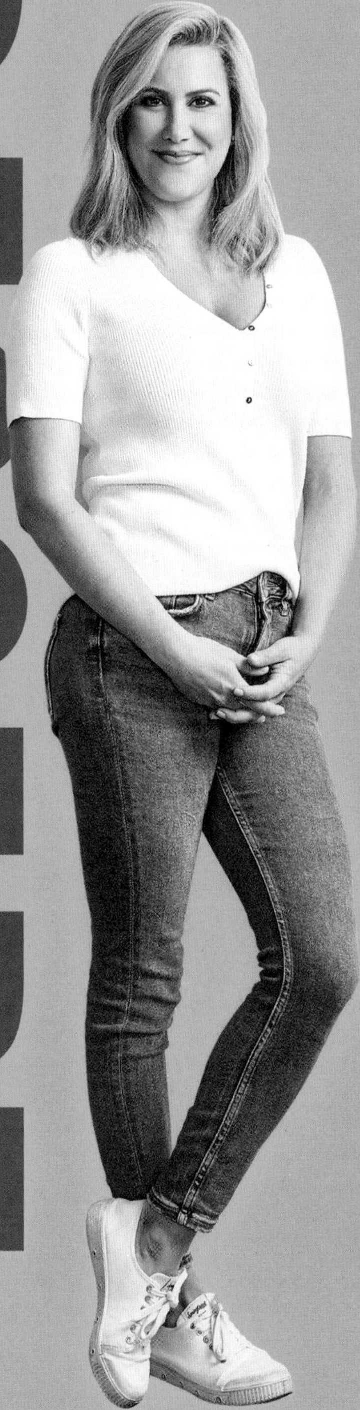

CHOCOLATE CRÈME SLAB CAKE WITH BERRY COMPOTE

This decadent chocolate cake ticks all the boxes when it comes to total joy. I love the idea of making this into a slab, rather than in a round tin, as the finished cake looks really generous and impressive decorated with the chocolate crème and berry compote.

SERVES—8–10

250 g butter, chopped and softened, plus extra for greasing

345 g (1½ cups) caster sugar

4 eggs

3 tablespoons black coffee, cooled to room temperature

1 teaspoon vanilla extract

a pinch of salt flakes

300 g (2 cups) self-raising flour

55 g (½ cup) hazelnut meal or almond meal

50 g (½ cup) cocoa powder

1 teaspoon baking powder

180 ml (¾ cup) buttermilk

chopped toasted hazelnuts, to serve

BERRY COMPOTE

500 g fresh or frozen berries of your choice

345 g (1½ cups) caster sugar

zest and juice of 1 lemon

zest and juice of 1 orange

1 star anise

CHOCOLATE CRÈME

180 ml (¾ cup) milk

1½ tablespoons cornflour

80 g (⅓ cup) caster sugar

100 g dark chocolate (70% cacao), chopped

2 teaspoons butter

150 ml thickened cream

1. Place all the berry compote ingredients in a saucepan over medium heat. Stir to combine and cook for 8–10 minutes until the berries soften. Turn the heat down to low and cook for 15–20 minutes until the compote is reduced by two-thirds and bubbling around the edge. Transfer to a heatproof container, then place in the fridge to chill until required.
2. For the chocolate crème, combine 125 ml (½ cup) of milk and the cornflour in a bowl and whisk well. Place the sugar and the remaining milk in a large, heavy-based saucepan over medium–high heat and cook, stirring constantly, until the mixture comes to the boil. Whisk in the cornflour mixture and cook over medium–low heat for 2–3 minutes until thickened. Add the chocolate and butter and continue to whisk until melted, shiny and smooth. Transfer to a bowl, cover with plastic wrap and chill for 1 hour, or until set. Combine the cream and chocolate mixture in the bowl of an electric mixer and mix on high speed using the whisk attachment for 3 minutes, or until stiff peaks form. Cover and chill until required.
3. Preheat the oven to 160°C. Grease and line a 6 cm deep, 35 cm x 20 cm cake tin or baking dish.
4. Place the butter and caster sugar in the bowl of an electric mixer fitted with the paddle attachment and mix on high speed until pale and creamy. Beat in the eggs, one at a time, incorporating well before adding the next. Turn the speed to low and mix in the coffee, vanilla and salt. Fold in the flour, hazelnut or almond meal, cocoa powder, baking powder and buttermilk with a large metal spoon.
5. Spoon the cake batter into the prepared tin and bake for 45–50 minutes, or until a skewer inserted in the centre of the cake comes out clean. Cool in the tin.
6. Once the cake has cooled, spread with the chilled chocolate crème and spoon over the berry compote. Finish with a sprinkling of chopped hazelnuts and serve.

SLOW COOKER METHOD

Place all the berry compote ingredients in the slow cooker and set to high. Cook for 3–4 hours until the compote is reduced by two-thirds and bubbling around the edge. Transfer to a heatproof container and chill until required.

Follow steps 2–6.

STEAMED MARMALADE PUDDINGS

These simple yet elegant steamed puddings are made extra special with the addition of orange liqueur. Don't let your imagination stop at just orange-themed puddings, you can absolutely change the marmalade for another spread like apricot or raspberry jam or even dulce de leche.

SERVES—8

160 g butter, chopped and softened, plus extra for greasing
160 g caster sugar
1 vanilla pod, split and scraped
3 eggs
225 g (1½ cups) self-raising flour
1½ teaspoons baking powder
a pinch of salt flakes
180 ml (¾ cup) milk
240 g (¾ cup) marmalade
2 tablespoons orange liqueur
boiling water
double cream, to serve

1. Preheat the oven to 180°C.
2. Grease eight 160 ml (⅔ cup) capacity ovenproof ramekins with butter. Grease a large piece of foil with butter.
3. Place the butter, sugar and vanilla seeds in the bowl of an electric mixer and mix on medium speed using the paddle attachment until pale and creamy. Beat in the eggs, one at a time, incorporating well before adding the next. Now add the flour, baking powder and salt and mix on medium speed until combined. Pour in the milk and mix again until just combined.
4. Loosen the marmalade by mixing in the orange liqueur, then divide among the prepared ramekins. Pour the batter over the marmalade until 2 cm from the top, leaving room for the puddings to rise, then arrange the ramekins in a large, deep roasting tin. Pour in the boiling water to reach halfway up the sides of the ramekins. Cover the tin with the greased foil.
5. Cook for 40–45 minutes until a skewer inserted in the centre of a pudding comes out clean.
6. Remove the ramekins from the tin and cool for 5 minutes. Loosen each pudding from the side of the mould with a small, sharp knife, then invert onto a serving plate. Serve with a generous dollop of double cream.

SLOW COOKER METHOD

You may only be able to fit up to six ovenproof ramekins in your slow cooker, so check before starting this recipe.

Follow steps 2, 3 and 4. Place the ramekins in the slow cooker and pour in boiling water to reach halfway up the sides of the ramekins. Cover and cook on high for 1–1½ hours until a skewer inserted in the centre of a pudding comes out clean.

Follow step 6.

POACHED PEAR & ALMOND CAKE

I love this almond cake as the addition of noisette butter and yoghurt makes the crumb super tender. It's made even more special adorned with poached pears. I find the pears poach better in the slow cooker than on the stovetop due to the even heat distribution. Once the pears are ready and have been removed from the slow cooker, be sure to reduce the poaching liquid to a syrup, as it's perfect for drizzling over the cake when serving.

SERVES—8

200 g butter, chopped, plus extra for greasing

1 teaspoon vanilla bean paste

90 g (1/3 cup) Greek yoghurt

4 eggs

230 g (1 cup) caster sugar

200 g (2 cups) almond meal

a pinch of salt flakes

100 g (2/3 cup) plain flour

1 teaspoon baking powder

double cream, to serve

POACHED PEARS

500 ml (2 cups) marsala or red wine

230 g (1 cup) caster sugar

1 cinnamon stick

2 star anise

6–8 (about 800 g) ripe but firm beurre bosc pears, peeled, halved and cored (bigger pears quartered)

1. For the poached pears, place the marsala or red wine, caster sugar, cinnamon stick and star anise in a large saucepan and bring to the boil. Turn the heat down to low and add the pear. Cover and cook gently for 15–20 minutes, or until the pear is softened and has taken on a lovely deep colour.
2. Use a slotted spoon to remove the pear and place in a bowl.
3. Bring the pear-poaching liquid to the boil and simmer for 15 minutes, or until reduced to a syrup. Pour over the pear, then cover and chill until required.
4. Preheat the oven to 160°C. Grease the base and side of a 22 cm springform cake tin and line with baking paper.
5. Melt the butter in a saucepan over medium–high heat and cook until foaming. Continue to cook for a further 2–3 minutes until the milk solids turn brown and the butter smells nutty (noisette stage). Add the vanilla, then remove from the heat and stand to infuse for 5 minutes. Stir in the yoghurt.
6. Meanwhile, place the eggs and caster sugar in the bowl of an electric mixer fitted with the whisk attachment. Whisk on high speed until pale and thick, about 5 minutes. Pour in the warm butter mixture and continue to whisk for a further 2 minutes, or until well incorporated. Add the almond meal, salt, flour and baking powder and gently fold through until just combined and the batter is smooth.
7. Arrange half the pear, cut-side down, in the base of the prepared tin and drizzle over 2 teaspoons of syrup; reserve the remaining pear and syrup for serving. Pour the cake batter over the pear. Bake for 45–50 minutes, or until a skewer inserted in the centre of the cake comes out clean.
8. Allow the cake to cool in the tin for 20 minutes. Remove the collar from the tin, place a serving plate on top of the cake, then carefully flip over. Remove the baking paper to expose the pear. Top with the reserved pear and drizzle on the reserved syrup. Serve with cream.

SLOW COOKER METHOD

Place the marsala or red wine, caster sugar, cinnamon and star anise in the slow cooker, stir and add the pear. Cover and cook on high for 2 hours, or until the pear has softened and taken on a deep colour.

Follow step 2, then pour the pear-poaching liquid into a saucepan and cook for 15 minutes until reduced to a syrup. Pour over the pear and chill until ready to use.

Follow steps 4–8.

CRÈME BRÛLÉE

When done well, a crème brûlée is a thing of beauty – silky smooth and just-set custard with a glass-like crust of sugary toffee. A quick tip: if you're wanting an extra shattering effect on the toffee, blowtorch one teaspoon of caster sugar, sprinkle over more sugar and blowtorch again, then do this one more time.

SERVES—4

2 vanilla pods, split and scraped

500 ml (2 cups) cream

6 egg yolks

115 g (½ cup) caster sugar, plus 80 g (⅓ cup) extra for the crust

boiling water

TIP—Transform your brûlées by infusing other aromatics in the milk. Some of my favourites include lemon verbena or thyme leaves, orange zest or cardamom.

1. Preheat the oven to 160°C.
2. Place the vanilla pods, seeds and cream in a saucepan over medium heat and bring to a gentle boil. Remove from the heat and stand for 10 minutes to infuse.
3. Place the egg yolks and caster sugar in a bowl and whisk until pale and thick. Using a fine sieve, strain the vanilla cream into the egg mixture and whisk to combine thoroughly. Pour the custard into a large jug and use a spoon to remove any froth on the surface.
4. Place four 250 ml (1 cup) capacity ramekins in a deep roasting tin and pour the custard into the ramekins. Carefully transfer to the oven and pour boiling water around the ramekins into the dish, to reach halfway up the sides of the ramekins. Cover with foil. Close the oven door and bake for 40–45 minutes until the custards are just set and have a slight wobble in the centre. Remove the ramekins and cool completely before placing in the fridge to chill for 4 hours or, even better, overnight.
5. When ready to serve, evenly scatter 1 tablespoon of extra sugar over each custard and blowtorch until golden. If you don't have a blowtorch, simply place under a preheated oven grill until the sugar caramelises.

SLOW COOKER METHOD

Follow steps 2 and 3.

Place four 250 ml (1 cup) capacity ramekins in the slow cooker. If you need to add height to fit all four ramekins, add layers of foil and a small wire rack to the slow cooker to reach the desired height. Pour in enough just-boiled water to reach halfway up the sides of the ramekins. Pour the custard into the ramekins, cover and cook on high for 45 minutes, or until the custards are just set and have a slight wobble in the centre.

Remove the lid and turn off the slow cooker. Stand for 30 minutes to allow the custards to cool slightly. Remove the ramekins and cool completely before placing in the fridge to chill for 4 hours or, even better, overnight.

Follow step 5.

RICE PUDDING

Rice pudding never goes out of fashion and this foolproof version is luscious and creamy. It is, of course, delicious as is but it's made lighter with the addition of fresh fruit, which I change up depending on the season. I like to serve mine warm but it's also fabulous cold the next day. Note: if serving cold, I highly recommend folding through some whipped cream or Greek yoghurt to loosen up the pudding and make it fluffier.

SERVES—6

- 700 ml milk
- 300 ml cream
- 1 vanilla pod, split and scraped
- 220 g (1 cup) arborio rice, rinsed
- a pinch of salt flakes
- 2 egg yolks
- 3 tablespoons caster sugar
- a pinch of ground cinnamon, plus extra to serve
- fresh figs, berries or any fruit of your choice, to serve
- zest of ½ lemon

1. Combine the milk, cream and vanilla pod and seeds in a large saucepan and bring to the boil.
2. Add the rice and salt to the milk mixture and stir through. Cook over low heat for 25–30 minutes until the rice is al dente. Remove from the heat.
3. Whisk together the egg yolks, caster sugar and cinnamon until pale and thick.
4. Stir the egg and sugar mixture into the rice. Keep mixing until smooth and glossy. If too thick, add a splash of milk or cream.
5. Let the rice pudding stand for 5–10 minutes.
6. Remove the vanilla pod, then spoon the warm rice pudding into shallow bowls. Top with the fruit of your choice and sprinkle over the lemon zest and, if desired, a little extra cinnamon. The rice pudding can also be served cold.

SLOW COOKER METHOD

Follow step 1.

Place the rice and salt in the slow cooker. Pour over the hot milk mixture, cover and cook, stirring from time to time, on high for 1–1½ hours or on low for 3 hours, or until the rice is al dente.

Follow step 3.

Remove the bowl from the slow cooker and follow steps 4, 5 and 6.

LEMON DELICIOUS

This easy dessert is perfect for a relaxed gathering when friends come over. If the oven is being utilised for the main dishes, I love to cook my lemon delicious in the reliable, steady heat of my slow cooker. Just before my guests arrive, I flick the slow cooker to low and let it do all the work so that later in the evening my perfectly cooked pudding will be ready.

SERVES—4–6

125 g unsalted butter, chopped and softened, plus extra for greasing

230 g (1 cup) caster sugar

2 teaspoons lemon zest, plus extra to serve

4 eggs, separated

75 g (½ cup) self-raising flour

375 ml (1½ cups) milk

80 ml (⅓ cup) lemon juice (from about 1½ lemons)

boiling water

icing sugar, sifted, for dusting

crème fraîche, to serve

1. Preheat the oven to 170°C. Lightly grease a 1 litre (4 cup) capacity baking dish with butter.
2. Place the butter, caster sugar and lemon zest in the bowl of an electric mixer and mix on medium speed using the paddle attachment until pale and creamy, about 1 minute. Add the egg yolks, one by one, beating well after each addition. Fold in the flour, milk and lemon juice to form a smooth batter.
3. In a separate bowl, whisk the egg whites on high speed until stiff peaks form. Then, with a large metal spoon, gently fold half the egg whites into the batter to lighten the mixture. Fold through the remaining egg whites until just combined.
4. Gently spoon the mixture into the prepared dish. Place the dish in a large roasting tin. Pour boiling water around the dish into the tin to reach halfway up the side of the dish. Bake for 35–40 minutes until the lemon delicious is golden and just set.
5. Dust the lemon delicious with the icing sugar and serve with the crème fraîche and an extra sprinkling of lemon zest.

SLOW COOKER METHOD

Grease the slow cooker with butter.

Follow steps 2 and 3.

Add the batter to the slow cooker. Cover and cook on low for 3–3½ hours until the lemon delicious is golden and just set.

Follow step 5.

STICKY DATE PUDDING

A slow-cooking book wouldn't be complete without a sticky date pudding recipe – the quintessential winter dessert that's so comforting with its rich, deep flavours of date and caramel. My caramel sauce is quite generous as I like to pour half over the pudding and, just for good measure, serve the rest on the side so everyone can help themselves to more.

SERVES—6

225 g (1¼ cups) pitted dates, chopped

1 teaspoon bicarbonate of soda

250 ml (1 cup) just-boiled water

225 g (1½ cups) self-raising flour

230 g (firmly packed 1 cup) brown sugar

1 teaspoon ground cinnamon, plus extra to serve

salt flakes

80 g butter, melted, plus extra for greasing

2 eggs

1 teaspoon vanilla extract

vanilla bean ice cream, to serve

CARAMEL SAUCE

80 g butter

170 ml (⅔ cup) cream

165 g (firmly packed ¾ cup) brown sugar

salt flakes

1. Preheat the oven to 180°C and grease a 2.5–3 litre capacity oval or rectangular baking dish.
2. Combine the dates, bicarbonate of soda and just-boiled water in a heatproof bowl. Stand for 15 minutes, or until the dates are softened.
3. Place the flour, brown sugar, cinnamon and a pinch of salt in a large bowl and mix well. Add the butter, eggs, vanilla and softened date mixture and mix to combine.
4. Pour the pudding mixture into the prepared dish. Bake for 45 minutes, or until a skewer inserted in the centre of the pudding comes out clean.
5. Meanwhile, to make the caramel sauce, place the butter, cream and brown sugar in a saucepan over medium–high heat. Cook, stirring constantly, for 2–3 minutes. Bring to the boil and season with a pinch of salt. Stand until required.
6. Set the pudding aside to cool on a wire rack for at least 10 minutes.
7. Pour half the caramel sauce over the pudding, then serve with the ice cream, the remaining caramel sauce and an extra sprinkling of cinnamon.

SLOW COOKER METHOD

Grease and line the slow cooker with two layers of baking paper.

Follow steps 2 and 3.

Pour the pudding mixture into the prepared slow cooker. Cover and cook on high for 2 hours, or until a skewer inserted in the centre of the pudding comes out clean.

Follow steps 5, 6 and 7.

CONVERSION CHARTS

Measuring cups and spoons may vary slightly from one country to another, but the difference is generally not enough to affect a recipe. All cup and spoon measures are level.

One Australian metric measuring cup holds 250 ml (8 fl oz), one Australian metric tablespoon holds 20 ml (4 teaspoons) and one Australian metric teaspoon holds 5 ml. North America, New Zealand and the UK use a 15 ml (3-teaspoon) tablespoon.

LIQUID MEASURES

One American pint = 500 ml (16 fl oz)
One Imperial pint = 600 ml (20 fl oz)

CUP	METRIC	IMPERIAL
⅛ cup	30 ml	1 fl oz
¼ cup	60 ml	2 fl oz
⅓ cup	80 ml	2½ fl oz
½ cup	125 ml	4 fl oz
⅔ cup	160 ml	5 fl oz
¾ cup	180 ml	6 fl oz
1 cup	250 ml	8 fl oz
2 cups	500 ml	16 fl oz
2¼ cups	560 ml	20 fl oz
4 cups	1 litre	32 fl oz

DRY MEASURES

The most accurate way to measure dry ingredients is to weigh them. However, if using a cup, add the ingredient loosely to the cup and level with a knife; don't compact the ingredient unless the recipe requests 'firmly packed'.

METRIC	IMPERIAL
15 g	½ oz
30 g	1 oz
60 g	2 oz
125 g	4 oz (¼ lb)
185 g	6 oz
250 g	8 oz (½ lb)
375 g	12 oz (¾ lb)
500 g	16 oz (1 lb)
1 kg	32 oz (2 lb)

LENGTH

METRIC	IMPERIAL
3 mm	⅛ inch
6 mm	¼ inch
1 cm	½ inch
2.5 cm	1 inch
5 cm	2 inches
18 cm	7 inches
20 cm	8 inches
23 cm	9 inches
25 cm	10 inches
30 cm	12 inches

OVEN TEMPERATURES

CELSIUS	FAHRENHEIT
100°C	200°F
120°C	250°F
150°C	300°F
160°C	325°F
180°C	350°F
200°C	400°F
220°C	425°F

CELSIUS	GAS MARK
110°C	¼
130°C	½
140°C	1
150°C	2
170°C	3
180°C	4
190°C	5
200°C	6
220°C	7
230°C	8
240°C	9
250°C	10

ACKNOWLEDGEMENTS

A beautiful book like this doesn't get made without the help of many wonderful people. Without my amazing publishing family at Plum and Pan Macmillan this book could not have come to life.

To Mary Small, as I've said in our last three books, you're like a fairy godmother. Caring, honest and always ready to make my dreams come true when it comes creating exciting foodie projects like this book.

To Clare Marshall, as senior editor on all of my books and after working so closely together on this 'baby', a heartfelt thank you for all the hard work, support and, above all, patience you have with me, especially when it comes to getting my recipes done on time! I just love working with you and value your expertise.

To Rob Palmer, my fabulous photographer. Always fun working with you. You not only take the most beautiful shots, you're also a great mate and food critic (sometimes).

Emma Knowles, you've been so instrumental in bringing this book to life with your amazing eye for detail. Going into this project, I couldn't image slow-cooked stews looking sexy, but you managed to nail it. Also, a big thank you for rescuing a few dishes that could've gone pear-shaped – you are a wonder women!

Dearest Lucy Busuttil, chef extraordinaire. It was such an honour working with you in the kitchen on the shoot. Everything was beyond perfect. Thank you for making the long shoot days so fun and seamless, and especially for keeping us all on track to hit our target each day. You're a legend, Luce.

To Naomi van Groll, thank you for helping to coordinate a great shoot. You're always so bubbly and smiley and such a pleasure to have around. I'm also so appreciative that you were always prepared to roll up your sleeves and help with the washing up – my least favourite job!

To designer Michelle Mackintosh, a BIG thank you for making this book look so beautiful. Slow cooking can sometimes look uniform, but you've managed to create a vibrant, fresh and modern feel. I just love it.

To Megan Johnston, my fabulous editor. Thank you for always finding those needles in the haystack when it comes to editing my recipes.

To the lovely Peta Dent and Delvene Michael, thank you for helping in the kitchen with the cooking on the shoot.

To Sammy Coutts, for always making time for me when I run out of time to test all of my recipes. Thank you for your accuracy and speed.

To my wonderful manager, Lisa Sullivan, for understanding that the writing, testing and all-round creating of a project like this takes heaps and heaps of time, and that's why I'm always so late writing back to emails! Hehe.

Justine
ox

INDEX

A Plum book

First published in 2021 by
Pan Macmillan Australia Pty Limited
Level 25, 1 Market Street,
Sydney, NSW 2000, Australia

Level 3, 112 Wellington Parade,
East Melbourne, VIC 3002, Australia

Design by Michelle Mackintosh
Edited by Megan Johnston
Index by Helena Holmgren
Photography by Rob Palmer
Food and prop styling by Emma Knowles
Food preparation by Lucy Busuttil, Peta Dent,
Delvene Michael and Justine Schofield
Typeset by Heather Menzies
Colour reproduction by Splitting Image
Colour Studio
Printed and bound in China by 1010 Printing
International Limited

A CIP catalogue record for this book is available
from the National Library of Australia.

10 9 8 7 6 5 4 3 2 1